THE NAKED HEROINE

THE NAKED HEROINE

JOHN IZBICKI

UMBRIA PRESS

Umbria Press London SW15 5DP
www.umbriapress.co.uk

Printed and bound by
Ashford Colour Press, Gosport

ISBN 978-1-910014-04-6

To those who, unlike Lydia, did not manage to return,
to those who received no medals but perished,
I wish to dedicate this book.

CONTENTS

1. Lydia's medals: Légion d'Honneur: Chevalier (knighthood); 2. The Insignia of Free France F.F.L. At the back of this Lydia's Resistance Number-38853; 3. Légion d'Honneur: Chevalier (knighthood); 4. Croix: de guerre 39-40 with palm. Croix: de Combattant Volontaire 39-45. 5. Croix: de Combattant Volontaire Résistant. 6. Croix: de Combattant. 7. Médaille: Deporté Resistant. 8. Médaille: Reconnaissance de la France Libre. 9. Médaille: Commemorative-39-45 avec barrette Libération. 10. Médaille: engagé volontaire. 11. Special Insignia of the Resistance Movement inscribed Lydia de Lipski, Lieutenant of the Group F—I Fighting France, Ravensbriick 1943-45 12. Croix de Guerre. 13. This is Lydia's Ravensbrück Concentration Camp number with the red triangle denoting the N.N. Block (Nacht und Nebel) and the black circle denoting the Punishment block (Strafiblock). 14. Insignia of the Federation des Deportes de In rue Boulin Villiers. 15. Insignia of the Federation des Déportés de la rue Leroux.

ILLUSTRATIONS

PREFACE

Newspaper journalists are constantly on the lookout for 'exclusive' stories – and some journalists even make the mistake of telling their news editors that a story they have submitted is 'exclusive'. This often turns out to be the kiss of death. News Editors have a tendency to sit on them, believing them to be 'holdworthy'. Only when other rival papers rush such stories into print are they considered worthy of seeing the light of day. Stories that can be labelled 'scoops' are, of course, far rarer than exclusives and should be kept even quieter.

Although I have managed to gather a fair number of exclusives throughout a lifetime of journalism, I can count less than a handful of genuine 'scoops'.

The first was my interview with a man who had somehow managed to remain unknown to the world, though goodness only knows why. His name: Paul Getty. I met him a matter of days after I had arrived in Paris in the mid-fifties to cover France for Kemsley Newspapers – a large group, which included the *Sunday Times*, the *Sunday Graphic*, the *Sunday Empire News* (believe it or not) and a host of regional papers throughout the U K. It really was an absolute chance meeting. I met a man who told me he was on his way to the christening of an oil tanker. I was still a little green and had no idea that oil tankers could be christened. He then told me of the man who owned this and many other tankers. 'You ought to go and speak to him,' he advised. 'You'll find him at the George V Hotel.'

And that's exactly what I did. When Getty heard that I was actually at the grand hotel's reception, he promised to give me 'just ten minutes'. We struck up an almost immediate relationship and the ten minutes turned into about two hours during which he kept me totally mesmerised by disclosing his life and many loves, his fleet of oil tankers and his money – lots and lots of money amounting to many billions of dollars.

The long and detailed feature I filed clearly failed to impress the short-sighted powers that be. Only my lead sentence – *'How would you like to be a millionaire forty times over?'* – made it into Peter Nelson's gossip column in the *Empire News*. It was a decent paragraph, which had summarised Getty's proud possessions, but it was not my 'scoop'! Only the eagle-eyes of some lucky guy on the American Newsweek magazine had spotted that paragraph and produced a cover story some three or four weeks afterwards which showed a portrait of Getty with a caption that filled every column-inch of space and introduced readers to *'The Richest American in the World!'*

'Didn't you write something about this man Getty?' I was asked by an embarrassed News Editor the following day. And when I told him angrily and in no uncertain terms that I had written some 1,500 words about him, he asked me to re-dictate the entire feature again.

It was, of course, too late to resuscitate my story but it taught me my first really important lesson to keep 'scoops' quiet – just like the one I saw tucked quietly away in the classified columns of *Le Monde* one Tuesday morning. It was a simple announcement in the French equivalent of our Court Circular, of an award of a *Légion d'Honneur Chevalier* (equivalent to a British knighthood) to a woman. Her name was given as Lydia Lova de Korczac Lipski and the award was in recognition of her bravery in the French Resistance. At first I pushed the newspaper aside but after about five or ten minutes, I pulled it back again and re-read the short announcement. Who, I thought, was this woman and what had she done to help the Resistance movement while France was under Nazi occupation? I searched through the other French papers on my desk and found the same brief announcement in the pages of *France Soir* and *Paris Presse*.

I decided to investigate further and discovered from the *Journal Officiel* that Mlle de Korczac Lipski had already been decorated with the *Croix de Guerre* with Palm and numerous other medals, including the Croix de Combattant Volontaire Résistant and the *Médaille Réconnaissance de la France Libre*. Lydia de Korczac Lipski, it transpired, was the most decorated woman in France. I was growing increasingly interested in her. Who was she? What did she do in the Resistance? And what was she doing now? I had to find out.

At that time, the war had been over for more than fifteen years. France was facing different problems, different troubles. Algeria was beginning to show signs of revolt. French expatriates who had made their homes there were campaigning for an *Algerie française*. The Nazi invasion of France and the thousands of marching jackboots along Paris boulevards were just a distant memory. So the renewed decoration of a woman who had worked with the Resistance Movement proved all the more mysterious. I simply had to find out more.

The only thing that was clear was that her name was Polish. I telephoned the *Journal Officiel* and asked their newsdesk what they could tell me about Mlle Lipski. I was told that she was a dancer and that she had already received ten other decorations for bravery.

I desperately needed a break and it came soon enough when the telephone in my office began to ring. My *Journal Officiel* contact had phoned me back to tell me that Mlle Lipski was better known as Lydia Lova and she was the top-billing nude dancer of the Folies-Bergère. Within one delicious minute, an interesting little story had turned into a sensational scoop.

The Folies-Bergère had earned itself the title of one of the best music halls of Paris, second only in reputation and excellence to the Moulin Rouge in Pigalle. It was the Moulin which had continued to attract most tourists and a goodly proportion of European royalty. Toulouse Lautrec, the unattractive little hunchback who had become one of France's finest painters and the Moulin Rouge's most frequent visitor and patron, also became that music hall's greatest public relations officer. Indeed, he still retains that unwritten title.

But the Folies-Bergère somehow managed to draw huge crowds of G.I.s after the liberation of Paris and American tourists continue to flock to the theatre that had become best known for its nude dancers. From 1911 onwards, dancers were allowed to cavort around the huge stage naked. There was never anything obscene on the Folies stage. Choreographers of great distinction produced ballets of beauty that brought cheering audiences to their feet. When Lydia Lova joined the cast of dancers as a soloist, the reputation of the Folies soared. Reservations had to be made months ahead or one would have to face disappointment or make do with the second-best – the expensive Lido on the Champs Elysées.

Nudes had first appeared at the Folies in 1911 and it created not only an uproar in the French Press but it also created long, noisy queues leading to the Folies' box office. The theatre's newly appointed director, Paul Derval, waited until the end of the First World War in 1918, when he had reached the grand old age of 38, when he went all-out to celebrate the newfound peace by producing a show that concentrated on lavish costumes and dancers who

[13]

2. At the Folies

pirouetted in the nude. Derval continued in this highly successful fashion for nearly 50 further years at the Folies. His shows were to feature such (fully dressed) stars as Maurice Chevalier, Fernandel, Yves Montand, the wonderful Edith Piaf and Charlot, better known in the rest of Europe as Charlie Chaplin.

In 1936, Paul Derval decided to attract Josephine Baker from her tremendous successes on the New York stage to the Folies theatre in the rue Richer, close to the rue Bergère (street of the shepherdess) and the Grands Boulevards. At the same time, he appointed Michel Gyarmathy, who was born Miklos Ehrenfeld in Hungary, the son of Saul Ehrenfeld and owner of a dairy in Balassagyarmath. Later, when the young Miklos had studied graphics and scenography at the College of Applied Arts in Budapest, he changed his name to Miklos Gyarmathy at the advice of a good friend, a woman dancer and singer, who told him: 'You'll never get on in life with a name like Ehrenfeld'. In 1933 when he moved to Paris he changed Miklos to Michel – and never looked back.

It is rare for two men to stay with one company for as long as Paul Derval and Michel Gyarmathy. Derval, born in 1880, joined the Folies in 1918 to produce the first of his many glorious shows. It celebrated not only the end of the First World War but also the start of France's *"années folles"*, which brought nudism to the stage of the Folies and eventually influenced the founding of America's Ziegfeld Folies as well as the Casino theatre at Las Vegas and the Teatro Follies in Mexico. In fact, Las Vegas decided to produce a straight copy of the Parisien Folies at the Tropicana in 1959. It continued non-stop for just about 50 years, closing its curtains for the last time in 2009. Derval died in 1966, aged 86, having spent half a century at the theatre that had become his veritable child. He was mourned by all who had followed him on the great stage of the Folies and by his many thousands of followers among the general public, particularly the tourists who flocked to the theatre during just about every visit to Paris.

Michel Gyarmathy stayed at the theatre 60 years – even longer than Derval – (from 1936 until his death in 1996), designing its posters and costumes and directing its dancers including the beautiful Lydia Lova, who forms the leading subject of this book. Not only did Lydia dance in the nude; she also acted as understudy to the Folies' many stars, singing their songs and even displaying herself in their acrobatic acts. When I discovered that the woman who was being decorated with the Légion d'Honneur for bravery and who had indeed been named as the most decorated woman in France, I simply had to approach her in my professional capacity and write her story.

Lydia was better known in the Fifties as the 'darling of the Folies'.

I expected to have an easy job getting her to tell me her story. I was totally wrong in that assumption. She answered my simple request with a shake of her head and arms: 'If you want to write about my dancing at the theatre, then please go ahead. I have no objections. But please forget the other matter. It is in the past and I'd rather forget it', she told me firmly but with kindness accompanied by a generous smile.

Sometime later I discovered that her objections were not only a question of forgetting the past. It was clear that Lydia would never, could never forget the many gruesome tortures and miseries she had experienced at the hands of the Nazis. Her reluctance to speak freely to me or any other journalist was because she refused to have the name Lydia Lova connected in any way with her real name – Lydia de Korczac Lipski, daughter of a Polish prince. The very idea that people might think she was drawing on her background for cheap publicity was totally abhorrent to her.

But after I had made contact with her father and turned him into an ally, she finally agreed to let me speak with her at length and write a short series of feature articles for my newspaper group in England. She had not the faintest idea – and in truth, nor did I – that my four articles in *The Sunday Graphic* would create a minor sensation and that, as a result, she would have to deal with gangs of hacks and paparazzi for many weeks.

The question then arose whether I should undertake a more detailed task: the writing of Lydia's biography. Again, she displayed the utmost reluctance – until her father decided to ask a family friend to make some discreet enquiries about me. The friend knew the editor of *France Soir* and put the question to him: 'Do you happen to know a British journalist by the name of John Iz-bee-kee? He writes for some big English papers, including *Le Sunday Graphique*.' The editor called a good contact of his – Ronald Payne of *The Daily Telegraph* in the Place Vendome.

And here we were back with coincidences in a small world. My own Kemsley Newspaper office happened to be on the same floor and at the other end of the same apartment as the *Telegraph* and Ronnie and I were good mates. I had passed the Lipski enquiry with flying colours and spent many weeks together with Lydia and her father in his Left Bank apartment, talking, talking, talking, taking a mass of notes and tape recording our conversations.

Whereas my *Sunday Graphic* articles had sketched a large part of her life at the Folies-Bergére and skated through some of her activities during the Nazi occupation of France, the details of her amazing life had a profound effect upon me.

So what was the sketchy part? It showed Lydia dancing to packed houses

3. Lydia: now she can afford a car… though only a Vespa.

of the Folies-Bergére night after night, being cheered hoarse and showered with flowers from American, British, French, Italian and, yes, even German admirers. Her naked body showed no signs of any scars. But beneath the greasepaint and the smile upon her lips lay the agony of a memory of past tortures and the many beatings she had endured in French prisons and a Nazi concentration camp.

One of Lydia's most famous dances showed her in a pas-de-deux with the devil, a physically magnificent young male and almost nude dancer, both of them cavorting across a blood-red stage with real-looking flames licking the edges of a deep pit in the centre of the stage hell. The devil plays a haunting melody upon a glass violin, whose tune is taken up by the orchestra in the theatre's own and very real pit. Lydia, a beautiful fallen angel, pirouettes around the stage, enticing the devil who, of course, falls madly in love with her. He lures her ever closer to him and closer also to the fiery pit and, as they dance together, the flames leap ever higher until these two hellish lovers are engulfed by the flames and disappear into the pit.

This particular ballet always proved one of the most popular with audiences at the Folies-Bergére. But to Lydia, who never failed to make her exit into the wings and back to her dressing room with the tears streaming from her eyes, that ballet brought back her most dreadful memories. It symbolised her past, her childhood. It conjured back the nightmares of Fresnes Prison and Ravensbrück Camp where she had been confronted by the devil incarnate and almost engulfed in the flames of the crematorium.

And when Lydia used to return to her apartment in the rue Hegesippe-Moreau, high over the rooftops of Montmartre in Paris, she used to drink a large glass of milk and go to bed with a prayer that this time perhaps, she would not be visited by those dreadful dreams of death. But they did come. They almost always did.

No medal, however golden, could have ever have wiped clean the past for Lydia or manage to interpret fully the true heroism of that naked dancer of the Folies-Bergére.

John Izbicki,
Horsmonden, Kent, 2014

CHAPTER ONE:

CURTAIN UP

The stage director replaced one of his five telephones onto its carriage. He had just spoken to Paul Derval, Monsieur le Directeur of the Folies, in his office. It was his normal nightly routine. 'All's ready,' was the stage director's only message. 'Okay, take it away,' replied Derval.

'Beginners please. Come on girls, hurry up. Curtain up in two minutes.' The stage director, standing behind his thirty-six complicated looking dials, switches and loudspeakers, sent his voice out to every dressing-room. Some of the showgirls screamed in mock horror. 'Hold it,' cried one. 'I'm not undressed yet.'

The 340 employees of the Folies-Bergère stood ready for another show to go on. Usherettes were hurrying the latecomers to their seats; programme sellers were persuading customers to buy the special souvenir booklet instead of just the ordinary programme. And how about a little nude doll that you can mould into whatever shape or position you like? How about that for taking back home? Seventy stage hands stood at their correct places, ready to shift and replace scenery within seconds. The eighteen electricians checked over the seventy-two switches that controlled the 5,500 lights making up the show and pulled down the switch 'Curtain Front'. The soft glow hit the crimson curtain in the front of the house. The conductor made his way into the pit to a faint ripple of applause, bowed, turned to his orchestra and — the overture was being played for the 1,214th time for that show.

Lydia Lova sat in her dressing-room on the first floor of the Folies. Beside her, a stack of unopened letters. The stamps on the envelopes signified that her fans were not only living in France. There were letters from America and Britain, from Italy and Spain, from Israel and the Argentine, from Germany and Sweden. Lydia probably used to have one of the best stamp collections in France.

The tall blonde whose slim but perfectly moulded body had attracted Folies audiences for more than eleven years, slit open one of the letters. She still had a good half hour before she was needed on stage. It was a brief note written in an almost childish hand and came from Germany. In fairly passable French it said :

'My dear Lydia—You will not remember me but I remember you so well. We were at Ravensbrück together. I just want to say how very happy I am for you that the French Government have recognized all the good you have done for France and for all of us. I read yesterday that you were given the Légion d'Honneur by General Masson. We who remember are very proud of you. Good luck to you, our little heroine, always and all my love —

Rosa Stern (No. 39486): Kiel.'

Lydia read the letter over a second time, her eyes filling with tears. Little Rosa. She remembered now. Little Rosa — the Jewish child who loved to dance. Poor Rosa. She would never ever dance again. Her legs had both been amputated in the camp. Lydia looked at herself in the long, well lit mirror. How long ago it all seemed — those years of horror.

It did not seem quite fair to Lydia as she looked at her greasepaint covered face, her rich looking plumes that she had attached to her head in readiness for her first dance of the evening. Here she was, thought Lydia, in good health, touch wood, still attractive despite her thirty-nine years, with a body that was envied by many a Frenchwoman and certainly by quite a number of other girls in the show, and yet she was being awarded medals while other girls — girls like Rosa Stern had to stay cripples for the rest of their lives and live only on nightmare memories without so much as a letter of thanks from some official at the government. 'No, it's not fair,' said Lydia to her image in the mirror.

The Légion d'Honneur presented to her on March 12, 1960 was her tenth decoration. She had already been awarded the Croix de Guerre and eight other medals. And yet letters of commendation had come from the very highest government sources, the last being signed by President De Gaulle himself. These honours had been paid to Lydia Lova because of her work for the French Resistance movement when she was a mere slip of a girl.

'Oh, but it is so long ago, all that,' sighed Lydia to the mirror on the wall. Three sharp raps on the door of her dressing-room brought her back to the reality of the theatre — the reality of make-belief. 'Five minutes Lydia,' the call boy shouted and passed on down the corridor to warn other artists of their cues. Lydia gave a little shriek of surprise. She would be late if she wasn't careful. Gyarmathy would never forgive her.

Michel Gyamathy, a small, thick-set man with wavy hair and an almost white moustache, was the artistic director of the Folies — the man who discovered Lydia. He was a stickler for punctuality and had, in his time, given proverbial rockets to such celebrities as Mistinguette (of whom the sculptor Rodin said: 'If I had to personify the Muse of the Music Hall, I would give her the legs of Mistinguette') and Josephine Baker, Maurice Chevalier and the immortal comedian Fernandel. To be late for one's cue at the Folies is a cardinal sin for even twenty seconds could have dislocated the whole three-and-a-half-hour show.

Lydia threw off her dressing-gown, touched up her tear-stained cheeks with powder, made a rapid check of the rest of her make up and hurried out of the room. The orchestra was already playing the opening bars of her scene.

The curtain rose upon a deep red, fiery stage. A staircase placed about half-way up-stage led to a realistic pit from which appeared even more realistic looking flames. Lydia, bare-footed, bare-breasted and naked apart from the traditional cache-sex — in this case a piece of gold and sequined cloth in the shape of a fig leaf — strode onto the stage, her long, beautiful legs cutting through the red glow like silver comets in the night. A burst of applause greeted her dance. The audience was not entirely unaware who this girl was. The few Frenchmen who were sitting in the circle or strolling in the promenoir — the part at the rear of the stalls, once used by the better-class prostitute of the area to pick up custom — called out *'Vive Lydia'* or *'Qu'elle est belle, la poupette!'*

Lydia did not hear the voices calling. She danced as usual. Perfect. Joining her dance was an Adonis of a man — himself almost naked, his body well oiled and shining to set off his muscles. He played a glass violin which hypnotized Lydia. This was obviously meant to be the devil himself, and the whole dance a *pas-de-deux* between this handsome Satan and the beautiful girl until, at the end, both would fall into the fiery pit that represented hell.

Few knew the symbolism of this scene where Lydia was concerned. She often had to dance with the devil as companion and had been to the very centre of hell. Indeed, she missed being burned by a matter of a few hours. For Lydia lived in a hell on earth, a nightmare that often returned to her

4, 5, 6. Reflections in the mirror.

7. *With some of the Folies Bergère Girls in the Wings.*

8. Ooh, la-la!

9. With one of her partners Michel Arène.

during the nights when she entered her small but comfortable apartment. Home for her was the fifth floor of the rue Hegesippe-Moreau, a modest little street that overlooks the famous Montmartre Cemetery to the north and the Place Clichy and Pigalle to the south.

She adored her street. Everyone knew her. La Mère Berthe, who kept a greengrocery stall a few yards from Lydia's house used to throw her a half-toothed grin and a cheerful wave whenever she came down to do her shopping. Le Grand Jules who gave up pimping in order to marry and open a little bistro round the corner used to offer her an aperitif once a week and recall the old days when he ran a highly successful brothel for German soldiers and collected information via his girls for the Resistance . And the girls themselves — they were still there, too. Josette and Colette and Jeanne.

Of course, things were no longer as easy as before. First it was the brothels that were made illegal. Then De Gaulle clamped down on the girls themselves. What was Paris coming to was what Josette and Colette and Jeanne wanted to know. Even the tourists were no longer the good business they once were. There just wasn't the money about any more. You actually had to bargain your way to a session. Bargain! A girl had her pride, when all was said and done. But, then, a girl had to eat too. If a customer didn't want to go along for forty francs, well, you just had to drop the price a little.

'Tu viens chéri? Je peux te montrer beaucoup de choses. Viens, viens…!

'But I've not got anything like 50 francs. Je n'ay pah 50 francs. Troh chair. Troh chair.'

'Bon alors. Mais tu as sans doute un petit, petit quarante francs— '

'Forty francs? You're mad. I'll give you 25 francs, not a penny more. Ventysank francs, non plus.'

How can you keep your room looking nice and tidy and your child well educated and fed when people just didn't have the money — or, for that matter, the inclination. Sex was getting cheaper, that's what it was. You can get it for free from a lot of those birds you see in them cheap dance halls and Self Service places. Self Service… Who'd ever have thought that you'd ever see Self Services in Paris? *Merde*, what a life when you have even Self Service Sex. Things were not as they had been in the 'good old days.'

Paris had changed. That was certainly true, thank God, thought Lydia as she wiped off her make-up after the show. It certainly wasn't the same. Even if the O.A.S. and the F.L.N. put together were throwing plastic bombs about all over the place and people were being arrested by the French themselves for shouting slogans and scrawling *'Algérie Francaise'* or *'Vive De Gaulle'* across Metro walls and all around the city — it was still better than her nightmares of 'the old days'. For they weren't the 'good old days'. They were bad, very bad, the days Lydia remembered every night when she put out the light and turned round trying to get some sleep.

At least, she thought, her son was safe now. He was growing up to be a real little gentleman and a wonderful artist. He'd make a great painter one day if there doesn't come another war, another dictatorship, gas chambers and crematoriums. He'd be safe. She'd see to it that Patrick would be safe. He was fifteen and being educated. She had never had the chances Patrick now had. And even if she could not really give him her name, he was hers. He was her son and she'd see to it that nobody would ever be able to take him away from her.

Lydia prayed, closing her eyes and clasping together her long, fine, artistic hands. 'Dear God, let Patrick be safe and grow up strong and healthy and wise and let him not make the same mistakes as his father. And, please God, dearest God, clean my soul of its memories. Please, please, God, let me not dream those dreams again tonight. Let me not dream.'

CHAPTER TWO:

FROM POLAND TO PARIS

L ydia de Korczak Lipski. That was the name on the birth certificate, registered in Warsaw, Poland, on January 8, 1925. The Prince Wladimir de Korczak Lipski had been pacing up and down the waiting-room of the Warsaw general maternity hospital for what seemed an eternity and what, in fact, was only six hours when the news was brought out to him that his wife had given him a daughter — by caesarian operation. It had been a difficult operation to say the least. Medicine was primitive by today's standards: Lydia came into the world the hard way and fate saw to it that much of that life was to remain hard.

Not that Lydia was not spoiled. Her parents were rich. Her father, a direct descendant of Prince de Korczak who was King of Hungary in the year 1120, owned three castles in the Ukraine to which were attached large stables, forests and estates. Her mother, who was reckoned to be one of the most beautiful women in Poland at that time, was a ballet dancer — of the classical school. But the Ukraine was Russian and the Lipski property was confiscated by the Communists during the Revolution. Castles and estates and horses and riches and high society soon meant nothing any more. The First World War and the Revolution had evened out the social scales.

The rich man in his castle, the poor man at his gate;
God made them high and lowly and ordered their estate…

The old Victorian hymn had been adopted and sung in Poland before the war taught the preachers and the people that, whatever its meaning, blood ran red in rich and poor alike and both could die for their country.

10. Lydia aged five months with her father and mother in Warsaw.

It was during the First World War that Wladimir de Korczak Lipski joined the British Army. The Poles are a proud race and a ruthlessly hard-working and intelligent one. It was pride and intelligence that made Wladimir volunteer to fight on the side of Great Britain, a country that was still as royal as the king of hearts and that still had all the jingoism of Kipling and Palmerston and Queen Victoria to lead it to victory. The British colonies were among the most respected and richest in the world. The Englishman was looked upon as someone to be trusted in any circumstances, whose word was his bond, whose power was supreme. The British believed and upheld traditions of all kinds; they had a heritage that could not be out-heritaged and had given the world Shakespeare and Milton and Keats and the little word 'fair'. Poland's greatest literary genius, Joseph Conrad, had joined Britain and had become one of her finest novelists. Wladimir de Korczak Lipski considered all these things and decided that if fight he must, he would lend his allegiance to the British Empire.

When the war ended, Wladimir was kept on the British payroll and, from 1919 until 1922 served as a full lieutenant in the British Secret Service under the command and guidance of General Carton de Wiart, who was at that time the chief of the British Military Mission in Warsaw. It was General de Wiart who later appointed Lipski to an official position:

'Prince Lipski, I have called for you today to make you a proposition.' General de Wiart sat at his large mahogany desk, twirled his thick moustache and cleared his throat. 'Your services have not gone unnoticed by our Foreign Office and I want you to take over as Passport Control Officer here in Warsaw.'

Wladimir felt a lump in his throat and an upsurge of pride and gratitude made him blush. 'Thank you, sir,' was all he could muster up at the time, although his thoughts went racing helter skelter around his brain shouting happiness and love. The British were fair. It was true. By jingo, it was true.

'Now, I'm not quite sure how you are going to take this, Lipski, but, if you accept the offer of this appointment, there's just one little snag. You see, to be Passport Control Officer, an Englishman ought really to be appointed. I've put your name forward, you see. But you're a Pole, aren't you?'

'Well, yes, sir, but....'

'So the only way round it would be to give you a British passport. You'd still be a Pole, ol' man, no doubt about that, what? But you'd be really one big step forward. You'd have dual nationality, you see — and British nationality at that. Not everyone's offered British nationality on a plate, what? Damn wonderful chance when you look at it. Damn wonderful....'

And so Lydia's father became British.

But the situation in Poland for the Lipski family worsened day by day. Aristocrats were not popular with the Polish people and were becoming more unpopular still — until those who used to take off their hats to a prince now passed him by without a glance. Later, they refused not only to acknowledge the upper classes but would hurl open abuse at them. So it was, too, with the Lipskis.

And that is why, at the age of seven, Lydia came to France as did many Poles and Russians and Ukrainians at the time. The Lipskis lived just off the Promenade des Anglais in Nice. Every day was a sunny one for the family. Lydia would run naked along the beach and let the rays of the sun burn her body to a roasted brown. She soon became the darling of English tourists who invaded the resort and whose financial glory had helped build Nice into France's leading holiday playground. To the delight of the rich socialites from London, Manchester, and Birmingham, Lydia danced pirouettes in the deep golden sands. Ice cream, lemonade and cream buns were showered upon her by kindly matrons in bathing costumes.

'You'll grow up to be a great dancer,' said one elderly Englishman in white flannel trousers, open-neck shirt and straw hat. From that day on, whenever anyone asked little Lydia what she wanted to be when she grew up, she would reply: 'A great dancer.' The Folies-Bergère, however, were far from her mind. She had never even heard of that theatre.

Since Lydia's mother had been brought up in the traditions of the classical ballet, she felt a natural pride whenever her hard-begotten little girl expressed a desire to dance and showed obvious talents in that field. Money was still no problem for the de Lipskis. Lydia was sent to an Ecole de Danse in Nice and soon showed a flair for dancing that surprised and conquered her teachers.

But Lydia's father wanted his daughter to receive a higher education. 'Nice is all very well for those who want to waste away their lives in gambling and dining and wining, but it's not the right atmosphere for a child like Lydia. If she wants to dance, she can always do so later on. After all, France is full of talented dancers. Every Tom, Dick and Harry is a budding Diaghilev and every midinette sees herself as either a Pavlova or a Sarah Bernhard. I don't want Lydia to grow up with any false ideas. Don't forget, we're not French. We're Poles. And whatever you may think of the French and their seeming lack of prejudice against foreigners, it's there. Deep down it's there. Unless Lydia learns to become a proper French girl, she'll never be accepted by them. Mark my words. She'll never be accepted.'

The day Lydia was packed off to the convent school just outside Paris, the world crashed around her feet. Or so it seemed to her at the time.

'I don't want to go. I don't want to leave you,' she screamed through hot, burning tears that splashed down upon her starched white frock. 'Mummy, Mummy, please... I... I'll die if I'm away from you... I'll die. I know I'll die.' And she wept loudly.

Irenka de Korczac Lipski scooped the child up into her arms, cooing to her, soothing her, rocking her just as she used to do when Lydia was a baby. 'There, there, there, my little darling, my little baby... it won't be for very long, darling... not long, I promise you. Soon you'll get used to it at the convent, my sweet, and after a while Daddy and I shall come to see you and, before you know it, you'll be finished there and you'll be able to dance properly. Oh, darling, darling, sweetheart, please, please don't cry. Mummy is with you, my love. She is with you, always. Always.'

Children soon forget their heartaches. And, after the first days of misery and homesickness, Lydia grew to love life at the convent. Nice and the sunshine and the beach and the sea — all seemed very far away.

Her mother had been right. She was not to be there for very long. On her tenth birthday, her parents surprised her. Mother Marie Josephine came into the classroom. Everyone stood up, all twenty-five little girls with their well scrubbed faces and their oft-washed blue aprons, looked at Mother Superior with childish expectancy.

'Come out Lydia de Lipski.' The voice sounded terribly matter-of-fact. Twenty-four faces turned upon Lydia as she slowly made her way down her aisle. What could she have done? What dreadful crime could she have committed? The children contemplated the reason for Mother Superior's visit, contemplated why she placed her hand on Lydia's shoulder and led her out of the classroom. Who could possibly continue concentrating on lessons when so great a mystery had enveloped the school? Maybe it was because she had giggled aloud during mass that very morning... or maybe because she had danced in the dormitory after lights out three days ago... maybe she had told something dreadful during confession and Mother Superior had heard about it. Mother Superior knows everything. That is, after all, why she is called Mother Superior. Some of the children silently prayed for Lydia's soul and that she would not be punished too harshly.

Lydia, herself, was also wondering what the nun's journey meant as she was being carefully but firmly guided along the corridor and down the long, cold flight of stairs to Mother Superior's office. I've done nothing wrong, thought Lydia. Maybe ... maybe something is wrong at home. Maybe my Mummy is ill. Or maybe it's Daddy. Maybe... oh, God, no. Maybe they're dead Oh, God.... The last words she half screamed out aloud and the old nun stopped in her tracks. 'Why, child, whatever is the matter with you? You know, you should never take the name of Our Lord in vain. What on earth made you cry out like that?'

But Lydia was crying softly now. 'Why, Lydia, Lydia! Why are you crying? There's nothing to be crying for. Goodness gracious, anyone would think you'd be happy to see your parents again. Oh, dear, there, I've said it. And there I was, meaning to keep my mouth shut and let it be a surprise like it was meant to be.'

Lydia stopped crying. The words the old nun had spoken had not quite sunk into her head yet. She must have misheard. 'My parents? Am I to see my Mummy and Daddy again soon. Oh, Mother, do you really mean it?'

By now they had reached the study. The door was flung open and there, before her, stood her parents. She had almost forgotten what they looked like, even though it was barely a year since she had come to the convent from Nice.

The Lipskis had moved to Paris and took Lydia home with them. From the convent, Lydia now went to a lycée in Sèvres. It was at this school that Lydia first took a real interest in drawing and designing. Until now her childish fancies had only craved for the dance. As she grew into her teens she became more realistic. To get on in the world, she thought, one ought to have something more than just dance. As she and her father would go for walks on the roof of the world every Sunday afternoon and look down upon Paris from the tip of Montmartre and the Sacré Coeur, she would look at the artists covering their canvases in the Place du Tertre. Her father would hold her comfortably on his shoulders so she could have a better view over the heads of the crowds gathered around.

She saw the Sacré Coeur painted from all conceivable angles. *Voilà*, le Sacré Coeur from the rue St. Rustique … and *voilà*, the Sacré Coeur from the rue Azais… and again, the Sacré Coeur from the rue St. Vincent and the Sacré Coeur from the rue Lamarck…. She knew the Church of the Sacred Heart better even than her own bedroom. And the styles! Goodness, the styles! Cubist Sacré Coeur, cut up into little blocks like the ones she used to play with on the beach in Nice; impressionist Sacré Coeur, wish-washy, haziness seen through the mist of white and blue and green oils; realist Sacré Coeur—just like a photograph without any heart or feeling but touchable; tachist Sacré Coeur in glorious coloured blobs dotted over large canvases; some few bearded young men were even painting the church so that it could not be recognized at all even though they swore it was there all right. They called themselves abstract painters and followers of some Spaniard called Picasso.

Wladimir soon realized Lydia had an eye for colour and shape and sent her to the Paris Industrial Design College. There, her teachers praised her for her rapid understanding of the subject and her skill with the pen. Later, Lydia looked back on that part of her education with gratitude. Shortly, sooner than she had ever expected, it was to come in very useful indeed. She also looked back on the part her mother had to play in her upbringing during this period. She was passionately interested in ballet and pleaded with her mother to let her take up lessons again. It did not take long to persuade Madame Lipski, for she had always spoiled her daughter from the moment the child was born.

'Lydia, how would you like to go to dancing classes three times a week?' her mother asked one evening. Madame Lipski was knitting baby clothes once again. Her pretty figure had rounded into full pregnancy, but her face had acquired a radiancy Lydia had never before seen. She ran to her mother and threw her arms about her for joy.

'Lydia, careful, or you'll smother him. Oh dear, you're not as light as you used to be — and nor is he....' And she patted the load she had to carry with a gentle hand.

'Him, Mother?' Lydia looked at the outlined embryo. 'How can you tell it's a he?'

'I can't tell. I just know, darling. Well, after all, we've had a little girl. It's only fair that you should have a brother to look after you later on in life, isn't it? You'd like a brother, wouldn't you?'

Lydia was still at that age when boys were of no interest to her whatever. She could never understand why men and women stood in long embrace at street corners. Men and women seemed to be kissing each other all over the place in Paris. Even when her parents took her to a restaurant, there would generally be couples who paid more attention to cuddling, fondling and kissing each other than to the food that was put before them. Silly, all this nonsense about kissing. Lydia did not understand any of it. So she just shrugged and said she didn't really care one way or the other.

'Tell me about the dancing school, Mother.' The forthcoming baby was quite forgotten and the very idea brushed aside. After all, dancing was far more important. It was certainly far more fun. Who, after all, could dance with a baby?

'Well, dear, I spoke to a dear old friend of mine yesterday and she said that if your father and I were willing, she would take you on at her school. Madame Stadtz has taught some very great dancers, darling, so you'll have to be on your very best behaviour. Some of her pupils at this moment are already stars at the Opera National — so you can see what competition you'll have. But — 'and Madame Lipski picked up her knitting again—'but I'm sure that, if you are prepared to work really hard, you'll be able to show them a step or two quite soon. You have dancing in you — just as I had it in me. It's in your blood, Lydia, and you cannot be rid of it. Your industrial what-is-it — design, that you have from your father. Dance you have from me.'

And so Lydia went to the Stadtz Dancing School and first saw the Folies-Bergère. The school was next door to the theatre and quite a number of the Folies chorus girls and boys still came to Madame Stadtz to carry on their dancing studies. Everyone had ambitions in those days to join either the ballet of the Opera or that of the Marquis de Cuevas. Very few succeeded. At least, thought Lydia, I shall be able one day to be the prima ballerina of the Opera. Though, she added in her mind, glancing at the tall, beautiful girls practising their steps at the bar, I shouldn't mind the Folies either.

The Lipskis christened the baby Gerald. His birth had not been any easier than Lydia's and he was a hefty, bouncing, screaming eight pounder. At first Lydia looked upon the new arrival as a menace. Everyone was looking at the baby as though he was certainly worth more than just a glance. To her, he looked just plain ugly — a red, slobbery face, with no teeth, a tuft of thin silky hair, all wrinkles and forever screaming. Why, he reminded her of the old man who would sit all day long outside the bistro in the next street. He must be about ninety-nine, yet he looked just like Gerald.

But, as the crying died down and people became more used to having the boy around the house, Lydia returned to her rightful place. Neighbours did not merely ask: 'And how is the little blighter today, bless him?' but also included her. 'And how are the dear children today, Madame de Lipski, bless them?' It made all the difference. Why, Lydia could even look at Gerald now. Before she was unable to get near him for all his admirers. She wondered whether anyone had ever made so much fuss about her when she was Gerald's age. Suddenly she felt quite old but wished she were much older.

Gerald seemed to grow bigger every day and as he cried less, he laughed more. Now Lydia looked on him as a real live doll with whom she could play. She even learned how to change his nappies and how to make him bring up wind. This new addition to the Lipski household was quite fun.

It was 1938 and the chestnuts were dropping from the trees at the side of the Seine. Gerald could already speak a few words. He could say 'maman' and 'papa' though Lydia was still a little too difficult for him. So he called her 'Biddi' much to the amusement of all the family. There was so little to laugh at nowadays. Monsieur de Lipski had a good job at the Mazda radio valve factory in Paris, but instead of his usual laughter when he returned home in the evening, his face would be grave. He and Lydia's mother would sit for hours in the evening talking in low voices so that the children — or, at least, Lydia — should not hear. Something strange was happening to Paris and Lydia's thirteen years could not quite understand what it was. People were quieter, more nervous and there was a tension at the Stadtz School that she had never before experienced.

There were now not so many pupils at the school as before. Many of the faces she had grown to know so well had disappeared. Michel Rosenblum, the best boy dancer in her class had left France she was told. His parents had emigrated to America and taken him with them. Yes, strange things were certainly happening in Paris.

Her parents who rarely listened to the wireless now always switched on to hear the news and made her be quiet if she was playing noisy games with Gerald. People began to talk of war and someone called 'Itler.

At the school the children were talking of war too. But to them it was not something to be afraid of. It was rather something exciting like a game of Cowboys and Indians. 'My father is thinking of selling the shop and moving Mum and me to the country... just think of it, no more school for weeks and weeks maybe.'

Paris Soir headlines looked bigger and more sombre than ever before. 'Hitler Marches into Czechoslovakia'... 'World on the Brink' 'Chamberlain Flies to Munich' 'The Jewish Massacre'. What did it all mean. Lydia grew frightened, not because she realized the consequences of war, but because she saw her mother crying and rocking Gerald in her arms.

'Mummy, Mummy, why are you sad?' Lydia, tears already threatening to burst from her eyes, ran to her mother who folded her in one arm and wept all the more. 'Ah, chérie, ah, ma pauvre petite chérie,' her mother sighed between her soft sobs, using the little French she had learned to perfection, for Polish was still spoken to a large extent between her and Wladimir. 'It's nothing, darling. Mummy is just feeling a little homesick that's all — you know, like you were at first when you went to the convent.'

Homesick? But for whom? This was their home, here in Paris. What was this talk of homesickness? Lydia felt more baffled than ever by this growing and mysterious sadness that was sweeping the household and the city.

For a whole year the atmosphere had not changed in the Lipski house. Tension throughout the world was mounting. Hitler was becoming a threat to Europe. In the summer of 1939, while the sun shone down on Paris and cherry and apple blossom lent a splash of colour to the fountains of the Rond Point, M. de Lipski helped his wife pack her bags. Lydia looked sad as she, too, was packing — but it was the baby clothes of Gerald, not her own that she folded so neatly and placed into a suitcase.

'Mummy and Gerald are going to Poland for a while,' she told her closest friend at school. 'Well, you see, it appears that Mummy has not seen her people in Poland for ages and ages and none of my uncles and aunts there have ever seen Gerald, so she is taking him along for them to look at. Gosh, I wish I could go with them. I can't really remember Poland at all. I bet it's a marvellous place, Warsaw. Oh, Ginette, if only I could go with them: It'll be a wonderful holiday for them. They'll be back in six weeks. But Dad says we can't afford for all of us to go, so he is taking me down to Nice for the usual four weeks instead. Huh. I'm so fed up with Nice. Gerald has all the luck — and he can't even appreciate it properly yet.'

At the station the farewell was a fond but normal one. Everyone hugged and kissed everyone several times, Lydia made one more attempt to ask whether she could go with her mother to Warsaw, and then the train steamed out to the accompaniment of handkerchief waving and see-you-soons.

It was the last time Lydia saw her mother.

CHAPTER THREE:

THE RAPE OF FRANCE

'**M**y Darlings,
'What an unhappy day this is for all of us! Warsaw has never looked as dark, and has never been as noisy. The Germans are just outside the city and Polish soldiers are fighting them to the death. There are wounded everywhere and we can hear the guns like thunder all round us. Last night we were bombed and, oh, the misery and the blood. It is awful, awful. I wish now that we had never left you and Paris but I am sure that it will not be long before we shall all be together again. I pray to God that He will put an end to this dreadful war very soon. They say that England will come to the rescue and that it will all be over in less than a month. God, let this be true. Gerald and I are quite safe. Yesterday I tried to obtain air tickets and fly back to Paris, but it was hopeless. There were at least two thousand people at the French Embassy and many more at the travel agency.

'How are you, my darlings? Please do not worry about us. This morning I went to Mass and lit candles for all of us. The church was crammed to capacity and we could hardly hear the priest for the noise of the guns and the wailing of silly, hysterical women. Gerald cried a little too but he was not really noisy.

'I suppose we must be grateful that we were not born Jews. They are the most frightened people in the city. They say that the Germans would shoot every Jew they found and that this has already happened in Germany. Can you believe that? I find it very hard to understand. I know that Hitler has been carrying out a campaign of persecution against Jews but I don't think he would actually kill people just because they are of a different race, do you? The Jews, I think, always tend to exaggerate their troubles. But then, again, they are used to persecution.

'If only I knew how you are, Lydia my darling and you, my beloved Wladimir. How we both miss Paris and, above all, you! I shall write again very soon. Meanwhile I send you my love and my heart wrapped in a million kisses.

Irenka, Warsaw, September 1, 1939'

The letter took a long time to reach the Lipskis. When it arrived, it was too late. The war had started and the Germans were already knocking at the gates of Paris itself. The Boulevard St. Michel was almost deserted. Small groups of students huddled together in the cafés surrounding the Sorbonne discussing the situation. The Germans would never enter Paris. Everyone was saying so. But as the days went by, optimism faltered. The German army was cutting through the veins of France and the blood flowed over the spring-time fields turning the green to red. And Paris wept.

And Paris wept still more tears of anguish when the jackboots crunched their rhythmical goose-step along the Champs-Elysées. Arrogant and noble, the soldiers looked. The Conquerors had come to conquer. And Frenchmen looked at Frenchmen and sighed. *'C'est la fin,'* they said. And men wept like women. And women prayed and lit candles in local churches and held their babies to their breasts and allowed them to bite at their nipples to draw away the last drop of mother's milk. *'C'est la fin,'* they said.

Among the crowds gathered at the Rond Point where fountains used to play a rhapsody of Paris, were groups who quietly sang the Marseillaise in a last gallant effort to show their opposition to the invaders of their liberty. And even their singing was silenced after jackbooted soldiers clubbed down their rifle butts on the choir's heads. Soon the singing turned to moans. And even the hard-hearted, solidly built concierges joined in the weeping. Paris had fallen.

Many packed their bags and made their way to England to join a young and gallant French General called de Gaulle who was mustering together an army to liberate France again.

Wladimir de Korczac Lipski, his eyes red from lack of sleep called Lydia into the living-room. The fifteen-year-old child had blossomed. Her beauty was the envy of the street. Chestnut hair cascaded over her shoulders and her apron clung to her well curved body as she left the good smell of the kitchen

11. Lydia aged fifteen–just before her arrest–a dancer of great talent and of infinite beauty

where she was preparing a simple but well spiced meal. Her smile vanished as she saw her father's face, lined and thin and pale.

'Papa, whatever is the matter?'

'The Germans are here, Lydia,' he said in a matter-of-fact way, trying to hide his emotions from his daughter. 'Now I don't want any arguments from you as there's not much time for that. I know a man who can get you out to Switzerland. You'll be safe there, darling. And when all this is over — and it will all be over very soon, I promise you—I'll come for you. I'm told things are very pleasant in Switzerland. You won't even have any difficulty about the language as they all speak French there. And Switzerland won't be involved in this war. The Swiss are never involved in wars.' He was adding up the arguments in favour of her leaving and the advantages of going to Switzerland. 'It will be like a nice holiday for you, out there. You'll have the Alps and the lakes and you'll be able to eat your fill. Of course, you'll have to get yourself a job and earn a living. I'm afraid you'll have to give up your idea of becoming a dancer for the time being — till all this dreadful affair is over — and maybe you'll even have to work in a factory. But as I say, it won't be for very long. Now, get your bags ready. There's very little time to lose. Don't pack too much. . Take the two small suitcases, that's all.'

While he had been speaking Lydia stood and watched his every nervous movement. She heard the words but could not quite understand them. What did he mean, leave Paris for Switzerland? Why on earth should she? De Lipski had only afforded his daughter the odd glance. The words skipped irregularly from his throat and sounded hoarse and slightly far away. Most of the time he had been staring out of the window at the grey-blue cloudy sky. Somewhere a dog was barking and someone was emptying the rubbish into the bins in the yard below. She had never heard the old clock on the mantelpiece ticking as loudly as it was doing now.

'Why, Papa, why?' Lydia could not believe her own voice. She had said the words quietly. Yet they sounded as though they had appeared from the bottom of a pit or inside some massive cave. 'Why, Papa?' she repeated and felt a little foolish, just standing there in her apron and holding a spoon sticky with the oil she had been mixing into the garlicy salad.

De Lipski half shouted, half pleaded. 'Don't ask questions. Just do as I've told you to do. Go and pack those bags. *Merde alors,* I'm your father, aren't I? Well, go and do as you're told — and do it quickly.'

But Lydia just stood there, gaping. Her father had turned his back on her and was now fully intent on that grey-blue sky that hovered over Paris like an upside-down sea.

[41]

'I'm not going, Papa,' she suddenly heard herself say. And she gripped the sticky spoon hard against her thigh and waited for the volcano to erupt. De Lipski slowly turned from the window and stared at her. For the first time she noticed that there were tears in his eyes. She had never seen her father crying before and the sight shocked her at first and then frightened her. She had heard him coughing a lot in the night that day he received the letter from her mother and she had thought then that it sounded more like camouflaged weeping. But she had done a lot of crying herself at the same time and paid little attention to her father's coughs. Now she saw the tears. They were slowly, ever so slowly, running down his cheeks and along the side of his nose.

De Lipski cleared his throat and blew his nose into the huge handkerchief that always made his pocket bulge. 'Look, sweetheart, let me tell you the truth. Things do not look very good for France. The country has been invaded and there is bound to be quite a lot of trouble. There may even be bombs falling on Paris as soon as the British decide to come and liberate us. Now this may happen tomorrow or the day after or it may happen in a year. These things — well, you never know. The last war took four years. Today, there are more modern weapons about and it may not take as long as that. But all these things need planning. I merely want you to go away from here so that you are safe, you see. And then, when it is all over, we shall all of us be together again, you'll see.'

His voice was choked but calm and kind and Lydia suddenly knew that she loved him. She loved him more than anyone else in the whole world. She wanted to tell him so but instead she said: 'What about you, Papa? What will you do? Why won't you come with me to Switzerland?'

'I can't, my child. I may come and join you in a few days but there are many things I have to take care of here first.'

'Well then, I shall stay with you until you have finished your business and then we can go together.' Lydia sensed there was something her father was keeping back from her, something he did not wish her to know, but she did not ask any more questions. 'Now I'd better be getting back to the kitchen or else there'll be charcoal for dinner.'

'Lydia, Lydia — listen to me… go and pack your....' But Lydia, beautiful, hip-swinging, coquettish Lydia was already humming a little tune to herself over the steaming saucepans in the kitchen. She knew that she had won.

After the meal which both father and daughter ate in nervous silence, de Lipski lit a cigar and blew the smoke up at the ceiling, watching it hit the wallpaper and disperse in all directions. He was feeling well. Despite everything he was feeling contented. The meal had been good. 'Thank you, my love,' he purred at Lydia who was methodically clearing the table. 'That was delicious. A stew fit for a king.'

'For a Prince, Papa, for a Prince,' she laughed. 'After all, that's what you are. Well, thank you, sire, for the compliment.' And she curtsied low before him, the *décolletée* of her blouse partly exposing her firm, young breasts.

'Lydia, if you insist on staying here for the time being,' her father said, suddenly genuinely angry, 'you must wear blouses that button up to the top of your neck. You must never let me see you in that thing again, do you hear?'

Lydia looked startled. 'But, Papa, I don't like those blouses. None of the girls my age wear those horrible things nowadays. They're old-fashioned.'

'Old-fashioned or not old-fashioned, you will wear blouses and dresses that button up. I'm not going to have a daughter of mine... I won't have people staring at you. And there's another thing. Tomorrow you shall have your hair cut short.'

'Cut short? My hair cut.... But, Papa, you've always said how much you liked me to wear my hair long. You're joking, surely, Papa. You can't mean you really want me to....'

'I've never been more serious in my life, Lydia. That hair of yours has got to be cut. I know I liked it long. But — well, I don't like it long now. First thing in the morning you'll go to Monsieur Bertrand and have it cut short.'

There was a finality about his order that forbade any further argument. Lydia, puzzled, angry and on the verge of tears, took the plates into the kitchen.

'Short hair high-necked dresses,' she thought aloud while she was washing up. 'Bah, *quel esprit borné*.' And she broke a dish.

But this round went to her father. The next day, weeping bitterly as M. Bertrand, Coiffeur de Dames, expertly snipped away at her curls, she was given a new face. She pulled out a thick woolen dress from the back of her wardrobe, pressed it, put it on and stood before the long mirror in her parents' bedroom. 'Well, I hope His Majesty will be satisfied now.' Lydia had lost some of her chic appearance and now looked like just another school-girl. 'Sixteen years old and look at me. I'm like a gamine at an infant's kinderdgarten.' Lydia felt she had been robbed of her womanhood.

Meanwhile, the Germans had taken charge of Paris. The Hotel Ritz in the Place Vendôme was occupied by high-ranking Nazi officers who drank dry the cellars and in their suites held parties that went on long into the night. German soldiers trampled through the Luxembourg Gardens in the sunshine and took the lift to the top of the Eiffel Tower armed with rifles and cameras like uniformed tourists. Bistros were crowded again—but now with Germans singing loud and lusty German songs. *'Wenn wir fahren… wenn wir fahren… wenn wir fahren gegen Engel-land, Engel-land.'* And *'Hinaus in die Ferne, mit Leberwurst und Speck…Das ess ich so gerne, das nimmt mir keiner weg.'*

The Hotel Edward VII had been taken over by the *Sicherheitspolizei* (Security Police). Steel helmeted guards stood at the entrance and most Frenchmen and women crossed the road in order to avoid passing the place.

France was suddenly divided into two factions. The majority of French citizens hated and abhorred the German invaders. There was something about them that reeked of arrogance and superiority. When they asked even the simplest of questions such as a direction or a price of some little trinket in a souvenir shop, they tended to spit it rather than say it. Orders to the restaurant waiter were shouted rather than spoken. A laugh was more of a bellow. And a declaration of love appeared like the overture to a rape.

But there were those Frenchmen who sided with the Germans. Rationing, which was severe and which was foreign to the palate of a nation accustomed to a cuisine which had enjoyed the highest distinction throughout the world since the days of Charlemagne, was perhaps the biggest burden that first struck France with the invasion. The promise of more and better food for those who collaborated came as a temptation not easy to resist. Financial remuneration for snippets of information was another and the betrayal of a neighbour who dabbled in black marketeering meant more food on the table and a thicker wallet. One forgot that a piece of information given to the Germans might mean the death of a fellow countryman — until one saw him disappear.

And there were *les putains*, the women of Paris street-corners, the prostitutes and the good-timers who saw in the Nazi uniform something glamorous, even glorious — something that had long disappeared from the French scene. In comparison to the smartness of the Wehrmacht, the French battledress of yesterday seemed dull and creased and unromantic. Military romance had gone out with the French Revolution of 1789 and made its appearance only in novels like *The Three Musketeers*. Here were young, blond, Aryan men who were fighting for an ideal — the conquest of the world and the destruction of all things impure. To many, this idealism proved romantic enough to share a bed with it. An additional bonus of a packet of cigarettes, some chocolate and a few francs merely added to the luxury of this sort of prostitution.

Who was there left to trust? Neighbours no longer spoke to neighbours in case their sons or daughters might overhear and report them to the police. The only place that was still completely safe was the Church. Those who refused to give allegiance to the Master Race, gave it to God instead. The churches, from the great Notre-Dame cathedral to Saint-Philippe-du Roule, were filled not merely for the regular Sunday masses but daily. And priests bore the burdens gathered at the confessional like albatrosses hanging around the necks of many thousands of ancient mariners. Eventually priests were made to undergo tortures at the hands of the invaders in their attempts to extract those confessional secrets.

And then there were the Jews. Or rather, there were not the Jews. For, overnight, the homes of those Israelites who had not managed to flee the country before the arrival of Hitler's men, were raided, ransacked and their occupants dragged away like so many sacks of potatoes to the boiling pot. The rue d'Aboukir's wholesale clothes shops stood empty, bared of their contents by plundering vultures. The rue des Rosiers stood empty, its houses silent and its strictly kosher restaurants deadened. The Place des Vosges stood empty and the columns that had held up its arcades over centuries wept with the crumbling masonry. The synagogues, the Victoires and the Nazareth and the Copernic, stood empty after the last Kol Nidre had been lamented and the last *shofar* blown. *Les juifs* had disappeared. Not many were likely to return.

All this Lydia observed but did not understand. To her, brought up in the dogma of strict Catholicism, nurtured on innocence and mixing at the same time in the artistic circles of Montmartre and the Quartier Latin where Negroes were just men with different coloured skins but the same coloured blood as everyone else and where Jews were just people with strange-sounding names and different dates for holy holidays — to her, all these happenings were simply incomprehensible. Her father told her that the Goldblums had gone away on holiday and that the Opatowskis had moved to Switzerland where he had wanted her to go.

And then, one day, she understood. She had just run down to the boulangerie for a ration's worth of baguette and was returning to the house, swinging her long loaf in her hand, when two German soldiers stopped her. *'Hey, Du, Du Kleine—toi, petite!'* one of them called and grabbed her by the arm. She dropped the loaf of bread and wanted to run away, but the soldier had a firm, compelling, steel-like grip. 'Where you go?' He held her by the shoulder now and spoke in halting, broken French. She could smell alcohol as he bent down to speak to her. 'I — I'm going home,' she stammered and fear gripped her as menacingly as this man's hand. 'Please... you're hurting me... please let me go home.'

'What your name, *petite*?' The second soldier had asked the question, almost kindly and was bending down low over her.

'Lydia, Lydia de Lipski,' said Lydia and added carefully: 'Monsieur.'

'*Was war das?* De what? Lipski? Lipski? -ski, -ski.... You are *Jude....* *Juif*, yes?'

'*Non, Monsieur, j'suis catholique,*' answered Lydia. She was really frightened now. A small group of people had gathered on the opposite side of the narrow street and were watching the spectacle of how to scare a child and give her a complex for life in one easy lesson. They were able to see a small sample of the Master Race in action.

'How come you've got a name like that if you're French and Catholic, eh? Answer. Quick.' The soldier shook Lydia till her teeth rattled and she felt faint. 'Answer. Answer. *Schnell, Antwort geben!*'

'My parents came from Poland... oh, please leave me be...'

'*Ach so, dreckige Polacken.* How do I tell you not lying to me? How I know you not Jew but only dirty Polack, eh?' And again he was shaking the girl. The people across the road said nothing. Nothing aloud, that is. They just murmured among themselves. '*Salle boches... oh, les salauts... assassins et emmerdeurs... oh, la pauvre petite, quel horreur, les salauts....*'

But the soldiers were themselves tiring of their little game. Suddenly, the arm-gripper pushed Lydia from him so that she fell against the wall of the house. 'Ach, you make me sick. All Polacks make me sick. *Zum kotzen macht ihr mich.*' And he spat at the cowering child. They moved off, but the second soldier had still one final trick up his sleeve. He trampled on the loaf of bread until it lay in the gutter, torn into thick crumbs of black dough. He spat into the dead baguette just to make sure it would be quite uneatable and then both men stamped off, laughing loudly at their little joke. If they had not physically raped the child, they had raped her mind. It was the beginning of Lydia's real education.

She lay there, wiping away the tears that had sprung to her eyes. Now she was surrounded by the onlookers from across the road.

'One of these days them German bastards won't know what's hit 'em,' prophesied one middle aged, thickset, generously bellied man with some six days' growth of beard piercing his chin. 'You just wait, petite, we'll get the swine before very long. The British won't let us down. Nor will De Gaulle.' And with that he was gone, just a shadow of a mass of other pedestrians.

Lydia had not really heard him. She was not listening to any of the sympathetic sounds that were being made by her compatriots. Her saddened interest lay in the tragic end of her loaf of bread. She gazed at it pityingly.

The others followed her stare and, one by one, the women delved deep down in to their shopping bags and baskets. From one a piece of bread, from another a few lumps of coarse sugar; a slice of cheese; and from another a crust of bread. Had there been a heavenly choir singing at that moment, it would surely have sung the Marseillaise. Instead, Lydia's eyes sang a whole benediction.

That day Lydia learned her first lesson in war. She learned of hate and of fear and of pain and of destruction and of sympathy and compassion. It was a hard lesson - but a valuable one. Laden with her presents, she ran as best she could up the flight of stairs to the Lipski apartment. She opened the door and fell in half laughing, half crying: 'Oh, Papa, Papa....' She stopped dead. There, sitting at the table by the window, was her father — and opposite him was the man who had spoken to her of vengeance as she stood weak and frightened in the street earlier on.

CHAPTER FOUR:

ARMAND AND THE LITTLE CHICK

'Come in, come in, Lydia,' her father said without trying to hide his impatience. 'And shut that door before we're all blown out of the window. Now then, I'd like you to meet an old—er--acquaintance of mine, Monsieur — e r— Armand. Monsieur Armand, this is my daughter Lydia.'

Monsieur Armand did not look quite as fierce now as he had done from the angle Lydia last saw him. He was not really as fat as he had looked in the street, but the stubble of beard had not altered in size. His eyes were steel-blue and pierced deep down into the very soul of the person they regarded. Yet they were kindly eyes and not at all the same as those expressionless, cruel death-mask eyes Lydia had perceived in the German soldiers.

'How do you do, Monsieur,' Lydia said politely and gave a brief curtsy as she shook the man by his large, rough hand. His grip was firm yet gentle. It was a grip that meant friendship and trust and generosity. At the same time there was a strength in that grip that suggested it could crush the hand it was holding without too much exertion.

'Why, you're the little girl who was being knocked about by those boche bastards down there....'

Her father, who did not know about that episode, showed immediate concern and Monsieur Armand and Lydia gave an account of what had happened.

'So you see,' said Armand to Lipski, 'there is still further reason why you should help us. You'd not only be serving us but also your little girl here.'

'I'm not a little girl.' Lydia felt hurt and wished she had never had her hair cut off. 'I've turned fifteen years and can look after myself very nicely thank you.'

'Yes, so I noticed earlier on.' Armand laughed with kind mockery at the defiantly pouting lips of the angry 'little girl'. His face grew serious again. 'Well, man, what do you say? I've not got much time for arguments and discussions. All I want is a straight yes or no to take back. Which is it to be?'

Lydia looked at her father, sitting there all solemn and grave, his fingers nervously fiddling with a pencil. What did all this mean? Who was Monsieur Armand and what did he want her father to do?

Lipski stopped fiddling and put down the pencil. 'All right, you can say "yes". I shall be happy to do all I can on just one condition.'

'Well?'

'That you take Lydia back to — er — back with you.'

'That could be arranged. You'll have to get her ready to leave Paris tonight though…'

'I'm not going. Wherever it is you want to take me and whatever it is you want me to do away from Papa, it's no use trying. I'm just not going to leave — not for all the party dresses at Dior.' Lydia was thoroughly angry. 'Who do you think you are, coming in here, ordering my father about and then taking me off somewhere I don't even know about. I am staying here and that's an end to that!' During this little outburst she had been standing up. Now she sat down with a finality that seemed to say 'you won't budge me from this chair ever' and folded her arms as an exclamation mark.

'Well, there's one thing about your daughter, Lipski, she's got pluck.' Armand turned to Lydia. 'I'm not going to take you anywhere unless you agree to come. After all, I don't want any little girl on my hands who's going to scream blue rape and murder at every street corner, so that the boche bastards can come and get me. They'd give a lot to have me under lock and key — and I doubt whether they'd keep me in a cell for very long. They can be quite nasty can the *boche* bastards, blast them every one. Now Lydia, can you keep a secret?' Lydia nodded, her eyes widening with wonder and excitement. 'My name is not really Armand at all. No, never mind what it is. As far as you are concerned, I'm Armand. Now don't forget, if you ever so much as breathe a word of any of this, it means the end for your father, for me and for a hell of a lot of other people as well. Understood? Good. Now listen carefully.

'I'm really a Pole. Like your father I came to France and from here I went to England with De Gaulle. In England we have now two armies from over here — the Free French Forces and the Polish Army (under General Anders). I was selected for — er — special work. I'm on one of these missions at this very moment. Your father is going to help us, Lydia, so that the war will be over more quickly and so that your mother will be able to bring your brother back here soon. Now your father wants me to take you back to England with me. I can see why you're not so keen to come along. Nobody wants to leave the people or the places they love and it's also one hell of a decision for your father to make. Now don't answer immediately. Please think it over very carefully and then perhaps you'll discover that your father's plan is really quite a good idea, hm?

'England's a super place, you know Lydia. You'll soon learn the language. The language is the easiest and the silliest but it's good and clean. And the people love animals and children. They love freedom, too, and I think, all in all, you and the English will get on just fine together.'

Armand turned to Lipski after his monologue: 'It'll be all right, just you wait and see.'

But it was not all right. Lydia did as Armand said. She gave the matter careful consideration. Somehow the fact that here, in her house, suddenly sat a spy, made no great impact upon her.

She accepted that part of the story quite calmly. Why should he not be a spy, anyway? Wartime is wartime and wars must have their spies — this much she knew from some of the books she had to read at school. No, that Armand was a spy did not really impress Lydia very much. That he was a Polish spy — this made no difference either one way or the other. No. Only two things interested her while she thought over his suggestion. The first that he wanted to take her to England and the second that her father was going to do something which might help end the war and rid France of men like those two who had assaulted and insulted her in the street. Would she be a hindrance if she stayed? Would she be of any use to her father if she left? After a good ten minutes' deliberation, she approached the table and addressed Armand.

'Monsieur Armand, I have made my decision and wish to ask your advice.' She spoke slowly, calmly and quietly and might as well have been asking what the two men would desire to have for their dinner that evening. 'If I went with you to England — and I know it to be a beautiful country from my geography lessons at school—I should have to start learning the language from scratch as you say. I should also have to learn to get to know the people and their different habits. And all the time I should be wondering about what Papa is doing, how he is getting on, whether he has enough to eat, if he is ill or if he has a pressed shirt to put on.

'And what of my father? Already he is all the time worrying about my mother and brother whom we've not seen for well over a year. What would he be like when I'm away too? Whatever he is going to do to help you win the war, will be done haphazardly because he will be doing more worrying than is really necessary. Now, if, on the other hand, I stayed here, do you think I would be in Papa's way? Do you really think I should stop him from trying to put an end to this war? Why, Monsieur Armand, I'm surprised at you. You saw what those Germans did to me down there in the street, didn't you? Do you honestly believe now that I am — am in favour of the war. Good God, I am as much against it as you are and, of course, I want you and France to win. Instead of showing so much concern about my going somewhere where I could be of no use whatever, think instead of something I could do here to help Papa and — and everything.' She had come to the end of her speech, performed with calm throughout. Not once did her tone of voice change.

Armand, a twinkle of a smile playing about his eyes and lips, rubbed the growth of beard on his chin. He stood up and bowed low before Lydia.

'I owe you sincere apologies, Lydia,' he said gravely. 'I called you a little girl before and you were rightly angry at me. You are not a little girl. You are a woman with a heart and a soul and, what's more important, a brain. *Mes compliments, Mademoiselle.*'

Despite her father's arguments, Lydia refused to leave him and join Armand in a British submarine and be taken to England. Submarines made frequent visits to French shores during the war. They picked up agents and British pilots shot down over France and saved by the Resistance. They delivered money and arms and radio sets. Armand made such trips fairly frequently. But it was not until well after the war that Lydia found out the man's real name. It was Squadron Leader Roman Czerniewski. He had contacted Lipski because he had been told to do so in London. Wladimir de Korczac Lipski had, after all, been a trusted member of the British Secret Service in Poland, was for a time British Passport Control Officer in Warsaw and had even been handed British nationality on a plate by General Carton de Wiart. The Franco-British-Pole was an obvious choice, Whitehall felt, to work for England.

What they had not considered was the daughter. Would she help? A snip of a girl? Very dangerous. Very dangerous indeed. When Roman Czerniewski reported the matter in London, there was consternation. 'What? A girl? Fifteen? Oh, now come, come ol' boy, you're bloody joking, what? 'A gel? Good heavens man, don't be a bloody ass. She'll panic... give the whole show away. Absolutely impossible, dear boy. Wouldn't be so bad somewhere in the middle of the country, but in Paris itself, no, dear me, no.'

Whitehall shuddered at the thought of a fifteen-year-old spy. General De Gaulle had just broadcast in the B.B.C.'s French service. Czerniewski used the speech in his arguments in favour of Lydia.

'De Gaulle has told the French to fight for their liberty. He did not just say that Monsieur Dupont and Monsieur Durand should fight for it. He appealed to everyone. And everyone includes Lydia. The Lipskis have heard the speech. They know now exactly what is expected of them. Personally I can vouch for the loyalty of this girl. She is highly intelligent. We've taken enough chances so far in the war. Surely, one chance more or less won't make much difference, will it?'

The brigadier and the colonels sitting at the highly polished mahogany table of the conference room pondered. They did not like the thought of a girl being given responsibility of this kind. Why, the very fact that she knew what her father was doing and was bound to see other agents visiting the apartment, was enough to make her dangerous. 'What if the Germans suspect Lipski at any time?' the brigadier asked. 'All they'd have to do would be to get hold of this child and put her through one of their third degree tortures and they'd have every piece of information they want. Personally I think we'd be fools to allow this child to take any part in this thing whatsoever.'

'But, sir,' pleaded Czerniewski, 'I keep telling you, she's no longer a child. She is as responsible as any woman I've ever met. And there's another thing about the girl, sir.

'And what's that?'

'Well, sir, look at it this way. Here is, as you say, a young girl — not more than a snip of a school kid really — running messages and perhaps doing even more important work for the Underground Movement. She looks just an ordinary, very pretty but ordinary, French child. Now, who would ever suspect a child of being an agent?'

'The Germans have got their Hitler Youth Movement, Czerniewski. They're only children, too, remember.'

'Yes, sir, that's true. But the French don't have such an organization. I don't think Lydia would be any more suspicious walking around the streets of Paris than your own daughter, sir, would be walking around the streets of London.'

'I suppose you've got a point there. But it still doesn't solve the problem of the father being suspected and the Nazis taking it out of the girl, trying to make her talk. What's your answer to that one?'

'Only as I have already said a hundred times before. That this girl is trustworthy and I doubt very much whether she would spill the beans even if she was captured. Anyway, you don't mean to tell me, sir, that there aren't hundreds of Resistance fighters in France who have no families....'

'Yes, but they're not active. You're suggesting this girl should take a leading part in the missions.'

'How many French children do not hear somehow or another what their father's activities are, sir? How many of them do not wonder what he is up to when he does not return home for a couple of days and nights? Is this not the same sort of risk you're running ? Couldn't these kids be put through the same tortures, asked the same questions? I can hear them now: "and when, my child, did you last see your father?" Oh, sir, I know I'm right about this girl. Why not give it a try?'

At first Lipski's job was quite simple. All it meant was keeping his eyes and ears open. He knew — and so did Lydia — the outskirts of Paris like the back of his hand. The positioning of existing factories, railways and roads was already known to British Intelligence. They were interested in any new factories opening up or, what was even more important, the movement of German troops, arms and vehicles around the French capital. Simple. Just a question of a walk in the country, a chat in the local bistro and the information would flow in soon enough they had said.

But how to pass on the information? There lay the difficulty and the danger. One false move and both Lydia and her father would have been shot as spies. The Lipski apartment became known to the Underground as 'F 1'—the headquarters of the Paris section of the Franco-Polish Resistance Movement in France. And, at the age of fifteen, Lydia (Lova) de Korczac Lipski, the future star dancer of the Folies-Bergère, was a member of 'F 1'.

Lydia's father organized the Movement magnificently. There were soon gathered together two hundred agents living all over Paris and its environs. All two hundred were directly responsible to 'F 1', passing their information along the line by word of mouth over a drink at the local or at the corner tabac. Once the information arrived at 'F 1', it was picked up weekly by a special agent who would then be responsible for seeing that it reached England.

There was the day when De Lipski was told that about 240 forty German soldiers had moved into a small village outside Paris and that there was something very strange happening not far from there. The Germans were building, they said, what looked like another town, but nobody was allowed to go near the building site.

Lipski looked at Lydia and then out of the window. The sun was shining and birds created a cacophonous chirping symphony along the rooftops.

'It looks like it might be another warm day tomorrow, *chérie*,' he said, puffing amiably at his pipe. 'How about you and me spending tomorrow in the country, eh?'

'Ah, *oui*, Papa, that would be wonderful.' Lydia skipped with happiness. 'It's a long time since we've been to the country. Where are we going?'

'Well, we'll see, shall we? Let's make it a surprise visit somewhere.'

The next day was Sunday. Lydia rose especially early and prepared the breakfast. She looked lovelier than ever. Her hair had turned almost golden blonde with the summer sun and was growing long again. Her father no longer insisted she have it cut short since his fears that Lydia would be raped by German soldiers were diminishing even if they had not completely disappeared. French girls, after all, were to be had in plenty by the Germans and there were surprisingly few cases of rape that he heard of. But he did make it a rule that Lydia should never wear deep *décolletées*. He did not trust the invading forces all that much.

After breakfast, Lydia and her father went to Mass and then took a bus to La Celle St. Cloud, a small but rich village that lies between Paris and Versailles. The bus was crammed with people but not many spoke. Some read the paper — German controlled now, of course — while women knitted their stringy socks or pullovers. Only when the bus passed German patrols along the road did a few men allow themselves the luxury of spitting out of the half-open windows. 'Hope they rot in their own shit,' said one, and this started the ball rolling — but not for very long. The bus was due to stop shortly and you never knew whom you could trust nowadays. Just one call and the German military police and French gendarmes would be aboard and the offender would be arrested, possibly never to be seen again. The Germans had concentration camps, people were saying, and apparently once inside one of those, one never again saw the light of day.

At La Celle St. Cloud more than half the occupants of the bus descended. A few stepped over to the one and only real bistro in the village and ordered whatever there was left to be served. 'Let's go and have a drink,' said Lipski to Lydia and, taking her gently by the arm, led her to the café. They sat at a table and Lipski ordered two rouges. The patron, of medium height with black, well greased hair, limped over to them with the order.

'V'là m'ssiedames,' he said and placed the two small glasses of red wine on the table. As he bent down low, he whispered to Lydia's father: 'Take the road to Bougival. Not far from the station, there's a road that bends off to the right. Take it.' He wiped the table down expertly with his cloth and was gone.

Seconds later he was back behind the bar exchanging gossip with the locals — just another bistro owner trying to make ends meet.

Wladimir Lipski took his time over his glass of vin ordinaire. Lydia did the same. In the little village square with its old steepled church and its unworking fountain, a dog barked. Somewhere in the distance a cock crowed. The voices at the bar and in the square, now whispering, now laughing, all seemed very distant, very peaceful — the sort of peace one finds when trying to sleep in the sun on a crowded beach in summer. The noise of crowds mingles with the murmuring sea and, together, they rock the sunbather to sleep. But Lipski could not, did not wish to sleep. He had a job to do. And so he fumbled in his pocket pulled out the few coins and, leaving them on the table, left arm in arm with Lydia.

Down the hill father and daughter half skipped, half ran, laughing and singing the sort of songs that fathers and their children always sing when on an outing. Nobody could suspect this happy pair as spies about to gather some vital information to hand over to the British. Up they went, up the long flight of steps that lead to the tiny station at Bougival. At the station, still echoing with bird-songs all around them, they bore right just as the patron of the bistro had instructed them. Soon the dolls'-house-like villas thinned out and they were in the open country. They had to walk the twisting lane for almost another mile before they saw the Germans. There they were, several small groups of them — and, sure enough, they were building houses. At least, by the looks of things, they were simply erecting houses. Lydia and her father continued walking, a little more slowly now, towards the building site.

'Halt!' The word sounded like a dog yelping with pain and Lydia's father swung round in the direction of the sound. Two German soldiers were advancing on them. Both carried rifles but did not point them at the Lipskis. The Germans had been having a little sit-down and a smoke in a thin clump of trees off the road. They looked embarrassed. They should never have allowed any civilians to come nearer to the building site than that clump of trees. *'Papière,'* demanded the first of the two soldiers, a handsome fair-haired lad with one stripe decorating his arm. He could not have been more than eighteen.

To him Lydia and the elderly man were just two ordinary French people who reminded him slightly of his own father and sister back home in Dortmund. But he had his job to do. He asked for identity cards, as a policeman asks for a driving licence after stopping a car that has accidentally overshot a red traffic signal. The identity card was the be all and end all to every offence as far as he was concerned and, when these were handed to him he studied them with the air of a schoolboy examining a Sanskrit manuscript. They were in order. He handed them back. 'You turn back. *Zurückgehen*.' And he pointed back along the path the two people had come. The second soldier, also young and brown from the sun, smiled at Lydia who returned the smile so innocently and sweetly that the soldier put his hand in his pocket, drew out a half bar of chocolate and handed it to her. Lydia looked at her father and he nodded permission for her to take it. 'Say thank you nicely, Lydia,' he said. 'Merci bien, Monsieur,' said Lydia and curtsied quickly as she accepted the gift.

'We come here for our walk every Sunday in the summer,' Lipski lied, pronouncing his words very slowly so the Germans should understand. 'What is the matter?' The corporal explained in a mixture of French and German that nothing was the matter. They just had to turn back, that was all. 'We build new village. Nice new village.' And both soldiers suddenly laughed loudly at this incomprehensible joke.

'Very nice,' said Lydia's father and also laughed, for laughter even in embarrassment, is infectious. The Germans walked back slowly with the couple and chatted about the weather. While they were walking, Lydia heard a distant rumbling. It sounded like heavy machinery at a factory. Her father looked casually towards the spot from where the sound was coming from. And then he understood. The jigsaw puzzle was complete. Over the fields, moving towards the cardboard village, rolled a procession of heavy tanks. These were followed by what looked like guns, long-barrelled, heavy guns. Anti-aircraft guns, thought Lipski. The Germans had also heard the rumbling, had also seen the approaching guns and tanks and had grown efficient. Their pace quickened. 'Quick. You go now. Quick, quick.' And they almost pushed rather than led Lydia and her father rapidly along the path back towards Bougival.

'Maybe we shall see you here again next Sunday?' asked Lipski as they all turned the bend of the lane together.

'Perhaps,' answered the corporal. With a wave the German soldiers turned on their heel and were gone — probably back to the clump of trees for another quick smoke.

What Lipski and Lydia had seen that morning was to save countless British bombers. The Germans had built anti-aircraft sites and camouflaged them as villages. These houses were literally made of cardboard — the sort of scenery used in theatres. Apart from the guns and barracks, all was prefabricated. The R.A.F. used to fly over French villages low and without fear of being shelled. They would never have bombed a small French town and only went after railway junctions and large factories producing arms or other vital war equipment. Had it not been for the immediate passing of this information to London, a whole squadron might have been wiped out while flying over this quiet little village near Bougival. And there were other 'villages' like that one dotted around France. As soon as one or another of Lipski's agents came in with a mysterious story of Germans building little houses here and there, the R.A.F. was informed at once.

One by one, these 'villages' were wiped out by well placed bombs. Not only did the R.A.F. destroy anti-aircraft sites, but they also bombed fair sized arsenals within them. For, under cover of these 'villages', the Germans hid ammunition dumps, tanks and armoured trucks.

This is where Lydia's training at the Industrial Design College came of the utmost use. As soon as agents turned up with the information of new sites, it was Lydia's job to copy to the minutest scale, the plans and locations of them. This she did, often at night by the light of a candle, on rice paper. Within six months she had produced the maps of more than thirty such sites as well as the plans of factories that were producing war materials for the Germans. One such factory was the Renault car manufacturing plant. Another was the factory at St. Denis.

Lydia, once she was fully accepted by the Underground Movement, was given a code name. It was the simplest choice to make and it was her father who made it. Since she was so attractive, a girl of fifteen summers, coquettish and ever-smiling, her now blonde hair having grown long again, she looked like a cuddly though slim chick. Her father, his thoughts still running in Polish rather than in French, often called her 'my little chick' — and so it was that she was named Cipinka, Polish for a small chicken.

To other agents coming to the Lipski flat she was Cipinka for all agents knew each other only by code names. Family details remained unknown to most. It would not have done to be too intimately concerned with any agent. The Germans had ways and means of making people talk and, whereas a single, false Christian name may not have been of great help to the *boche*, correct names meant immediate arrest and the break-up and destruction of a whole movement.

Cipinka's life at this stage had not changed openly. She was still continuing with her dancing classes in the vicinity of the Folies-Bergère. Most of the other students there had joined the Resistance and many were members of 'F 1'. While Lydia danced, her father was hard at work at the Mazda Radio Factory producing valves. But he was even busier planning and directing the sabotage of machinery at this and other factories and at night, while

Lydia was copying out plans on rice paper, he directed attacks on German installations. He and a band of friends took grave risks placing powerful time bombs. The Germans were becoming more and more bewildered and angry as they found their bridges blown up and their factories crippled through saboteurs. They could not continually send the same excuse to Berlin— that it was the R.A.F. that had bombed them.

When Adolf Hitler drove through Paris in 1941, he smiled across at the Eiffel Tower from the Trocadéro fountains while the bands played martial music in his honour. The Fuehrer secretly insisted that the French Underground Movement be stamped out and stamped out fast. The German commandant of Paris, during his interview with Hitler, was given this warning:

'It is ridiculous that you should allow these stupid French ruffians to twist you round their little fingers. Either you destroy them or I shall destroy you. Is that clearly understood.' Hitler was furious. He had wanted Paris almost as dearly as he wanted London and Moscow. He loved Paris and wanted the French capital to remain intact. He knew the Allies would not dare bomb this beauty spot of the world and he had no desire to destroy it either. That bombs were exploding not only inside the city but at vital military installations and that these bombs had been placed there by civilians who knew nothing about army tactics, was a disgrace. This he would not allow, would never tolerate.

'How you do it is your affair. Take hostages. Shoot them in the public squares. Do anything you like but catch me these foul heretics, these maniacs, these fools.' Hitler sat down, breathing heavily, his eyes blazing anger and his hand trembling. He quickly worked himself into a temper of emotions. The interview was at an end. Paris would have to be conquered all over again.

CHAPTER FIVE:

DANCING WITH DEATH

'Lydia, I want to talk to you a moment.' Georges was a good-looking young man in his early twenties and was one of the most promising of the dancers at the school. He had caught up with Lydia as she was making her way home and now led her by the arm to a little café on the Boulevard Poissonnière. Georges never looked happy, his finely chiselled face, pale and sad now appeared more intent than ever.

'Listen, I've an idea. How would you like to help me form a dancing group? I've been planning this for a long time now. Everything is completely organized — everything that is except the one thing we need most — the dancers. I've found a little theatre up in Pigalle and they've told me I could have it. It's closed down at the moment anyway, so it might as well be given to us as to anyone else. The stage is not terribly big but it'll do. If we could form a group of just a dozen. A dozen would be perfect, really. We won't need many more than that and....'

'Hey, wait a minute. You're rattling away so fast I'm losing track. Slow down Georges or you'll do yourself an injury.' Lydia was amused. She had never heard Georges speak so much in so short a space of time.

But Georges took no notice of her smiling objection. 'Look, this is important. Believe me, it's important. We've got to do something and this is the best way. Don't you see? We'll be able to make some money at it too. And we can put on a whole repertoire of ballets. Not just the old classical stuff. We'll be able to — well, maybe dance to something more up-to-date. I've been thinking. Some of the modern French songs — well, if we take a whole pile of them and have them arranged — I've even got someone who'll be willing to write the arrangements and play for us as well — I mean, well, damn it, it'll be great. And I want you to dance the lead. How about that? My little ballerina, my little Cipinka?' He stopped suddenly and looked embarrassed.

Lydia stared at him for a long time. She felt very confused. How on earth did Georges know? Who had told him? What did all this mean? But, although she wanted to ask him all these questions, she remained silent.

'I'm sorry, I should not have said that,' whispered Georges and his eyes begged forgiveness and flashed sadness. 'I — I know, you see. That is well, I'm also. I'm also in the Movement,' he finally blurted out. It appeared Georges was a member of the same group as Lydia — only he came under 'F 4' and had never yet had the chance to come into contact with Lydia at the Lipski flat.

Lydia knew Georges was speaking the truth. She could tell by looking into his eyes. He was the sort of boy who, if he told a lie, however small, his eyes would look down upon the ground and he would blush. But, even though she believed him, she said nothing. It was no use taking any undue risks these days.

After a while Lydia said: 'And what of this theatre? Why this sudden desire to give public performances?'

'Well, for one thing, we could make money. We don't have to charge very much but just enough to pay for the rent of the theatre and have a bit to put aside. That bit will come in very useful. I'll explain. Who are the people who go most often to the theatre nowadays? Why, the Germans of course. So, maybe the Germans will come to watch us. They may even like us. Lydia looked at him, and did not hide her disgust at the idea of having Germans watching her dance. 'I'm sorry, Georges, but I really don't feel like dancing in front of the Germans, thank you.' She half stood up and made to go. But Georges pulled her back down onto her chair. 'You little fool. You really don't understand, do you?'

'No, I don't. What is there to understand?'

'Good God girl, don't you see? If the boche comes to see us and they pay, well then their money will actually be used later to help the cause.

'Think of the extra food we could give to some poor *copain* ('pal') — Georges referred to an Englishman or other ally in need. Anyway, think it over — and let me have the answer tomorrow.' And with a gentle backslap of comradeship, Georges was gone, leaving a somewhat bewildered Lydia staring after his shadow. The idea of actually dancing on a real stage with a real audience to applaud them — this appealed to her. After all, her mother used to do it, and Lydia was born with the theatre in her blood. She felt her face flush with excitement. This seemed to be the moment she had always dreamed about. But, the idea of having to dance in front of Germans — this was another matter. Lydia did not like the Germans. She had never forgotten the incident in the street that day. No matter what she heard some people saying about the *boche* — and there were certainly enough in Paris who thought the Germans were all right — they would always remain her enemies as long as they occupied France. The announcer on the B.B.C. to whom she and her father listened regularly, had said only the previous evening that it would not be long before the Allies would liberate Europe from the Nazis. It did not seem fair to be planning their entertainment while others were planning their downfall.

And yet the idea had nevertheless made its desired impact and by the time she arrived home, had prepared the meal and set the table, she was convinced that, in this way, she could best serve France.

Her father, instead of refusing to give his permission to the venture, as she had feared, seemed delighted with it and gave it his blessing. And so the Polish Ballet of Pigalle was formed. Most of the members of this young troupe were Polish, a few were French, but all were trusted members of the Resistance. It was not long before the little theatre of the Boulevard de Clichy was almost filled to capacity by German officers and soldiers. The Germans have always been a romantic race, despite their forced return to the classical era of ancient Rome. Young Germans had been brought up on Nietzsche and military marches but their parents still took them to the opera to hear Wagner, and no German could consider himself fully educated without having learned to appreciate the ballet. Some even continued to read Heinrich Heine in secret even though he was a Jew and his works had been publicly burned.

The ballet company was an almost immediate success. Word had spread quickly through the officer ranks of the army. And they booked their tickets from general down to lieutenant. The stalls were taken up by Germans eager to hear the music of Debussy played on two pianos, a handful of violins, three trumpets, percussion and one cello or, when they were obtainable, records played over an amplifier. They cheered the dancers generously and sincerely. Some of the younger officers even tried to date the prettier girls of the troupe. Lydia was showered with flowers every night and visiting cards were often brought to her tiny dressing-room.

'Leutnant Kurt Hegelmann presents his compliments and would the Mademoiselle do him the honour of dining with him after her delightful performance.' German manners were never forgotten and the equally polite refusals Lydia sent back, excusing herself because of tiredness, headache, prior engagement or sickness in the family, were accepted in good grace.

While Lydia was dancing, her father was hard at work, directing attacks on German installations and the sabotage of factory machines. And when she returned home, she would begin on her second job — her real work as she considered it — the careful and meticulously accurate copying of plans that were to be sent to England. They were taken out of the Lipski flat by devious means. Some were secreted inside lipstick cases. Others went into packets of razor blades. And others were hidden inside the leather buttons of an overcoat. The buttons were hollow and would unscrew into two neat sections. Messages written on rice paper together with maps or plans of enemy camps, hide-outs, depots and the like easily folded into tiny balls of paper to be placed into the button. Lipstick cases had false bottoms and there were even toothbrushes that unscrewed at the bristles to hold messages.

Lydia knew the risk she was running by remaining at the flat and performing the highly demanding task of copying plans to scale. She knew her home might be raided any day. She knew that the penalty for spying was death.

But she neither cared nor worried about these dreadful consequences. She enjoyed her work, felt she was doing something to help bring about a quick ending to this senseless war, help bring her mother and brother back from an ominously silent Poland, help her country which had been trampled under the jackboot. Her eyes grew weak from working by the ill rays of light thrown from a 25-watt bulb, but bright lights in the middle of the night were suspected. Although the windows of the flat were well blacked out according to the regulations, German patrols had a nasty habit of stealing quietly up the stairs of the Paris tenements in the middle of the night to see whether any cracks of light filtered underneath apartment doors. Then would come the loud hammering of knuckle against wood accompanied by the shrill hysterically screamed command: *'Sofort aufmachen!'* and the flat would be ransacked in a search for hidden arms, radios and the like — even if the light had only been shining for some sick child in the family.

Later, when the Polish Ballet of Pigalle had been established for some months, and 'F 1' was becoming a veritable den of spies with messages being run hither and thither ten or fifteen times a day, Lydia's courage grew. The Germans sitting so comfortably in the small theatre, smoking cigars and chewing chocolate, would not have cheered so loudly in appreciation of the dancers if they had known about their Resistance work.

The stalls were filled with Germans. The tiny circle, however, was not considered good enough for them. When seats there had been offered to them at the beginning, after the stalls had all been booked up, they were refused. And so, gradually, it became a 'tradition' that the 'gods' would be reserved for the French. And among those Frenchmen and women often sat British and Polish pilots and crews of R.A.F. airplanes shot down over France. Those who were not killed in the crash or were not taken prisoner after parachuting to earth, were picked up by the Maquis, hidden and rested for a while and then handed over to special agents of the Resistance. Lydia and her father were among those who falsified identity papers for these escapees from death and P.O.W. camps. They were hidden away in the cellar of the Lipski house, together with the arms, time-bombs and other sabotage equipment awaiting transport to the coast. If they were not caught on the way, they were met there by a British submarine and taken back to England. 'Blighty' was one of the first English words Lydia ever learned.

There was, for instance James ('Jock') Andrews. He had been shot down over France while returning from a bombing raid on Cologne. Shrapnel had pierced his chest and he was unconscious when he was discovered by a farmer and his wife. After extracting him from his parachute and burning it, they took him to their hay loft. Jock, when he came to, was in a high fever and screaming with the pain. The golden hay turned red from his blood.

The farmer was a trusted member of the Resistance — but the doctor at the nearest village was not. It was suspected that he was working for the Germans — and after the war, he was executed. The only man to be trusted was the local veterinary surgeon, one Marcel Delacroix, an old man, whose experience of operations went back to the day he qualified thirty-four years earlier. And those operations had been carried out on horses, pregnant cows and the odd dog. He had never actually used a scalpel on a human being. He came at once to the farm together with his little black bag and examined the dying pilot for a full five minutes. His spectacles slid to the end of his nose and his hands trembled slightly as he laid them on Jock's chest. The hypodermic he used had only ever pierced the skin of an animal bigger and tougher than this young, handsome Scot's, but Delacroix used it as gently as if the man were a newly-born lamb. After quietly asking for some hot water, Delacroix worked in silence, extracting the splinters of shrapnel lodged in the boy's chest, cleaning out the gaping wound, stitching it up and bandaging it. Delacroix saved the Englishman's life. While the operation was in progress, three other members of Jock's crew approached the farm, dazed and bewildered to find themselves on strange land, frightened lest they should be captured by the Germans. They planned to take the farm by surprise, kill the occupants if need be and gather together enough food to last them a few days — and some clothes.

Much to their surprise and relief they found themselves among friends. Two weeks later they were all in Lydia Lipski's apartment, tasting simple but good cooking and waiting for a courier to take them back to the coast and 'Blighty'. They were among the audience at Lydia's little theatre and cheered as wildly as the Frenchmen around them and louder than any of the Germans below.

The cellars in which they slept and ate during most of their five-day stay, belonged to Madame Marthe Berteaux, a dear friend of the Lipskis. She, too, ran the risk of death, not only for helping to hide enemies of the occupying powers, but for keeping in those cellars the arms, ammunition and the printing press used for forging documents. It was here that young Lydia and her father produced ration and identity cards for the men on the run. Lydia's skill again proved invaluable, for it was she who wrote out the names and false addresses and forged the signatures of the officials over the forged rubber stamps produced in yet another section of the Movement. Madame Berteaux continued to live in that same house for many years and would recall with great pride the work that Lydia used to do.

Hardly any of the Britons and Poles who were kept by the Lipskis spoke French. That is why each man had to be accompanied by a special agent wherever he went. It would not have done for an Englishman to be found walking the streets of Paris by himself in those days. To these men, Lydia was nurse, sister, maid and guardian angel. After 'Blighty', she learned the words: 'I love you.' They were repeated to her time and again.

'Hey, Lydia, darling, come here a minute. I want to tell you something. I — love — you. Go on, have a bash and say it. I — love — you.'

'Oh, ça va, ça va,' and Lydia would laugh her usual reply.

'Sah-vah, sah-vah is that all you ever say?' But the boys forgave her. They knew she was too busy trying to save their lives to bother about love. There was no time for love in those days. And so the hidden strangers from across the sea contented themselves by thoughts of home. Lydia would listen to their tales of wife and children for hours on end. The men told her everything. Of how they loved their wives in London or Coventry or Cardiff; how many children they had; how many more children they were going to have when all this was over; they told her about the pub at the corner and the number of pints they would buy as soon as they returned there; they told her of their troubles and their worries and their dreams. They told her everything and she listened to them while she worked on at some document. Why should she not hear their confessions? She could not understand a single word. Not a single word.

And when they were taken away, one by one, to return to England, taken away mainly in lorries that delivered vegetables to Les Halles market and made their return journey to the country at dawn, the men promised Lydia their never-dying devotion. 'After the war, darling, we'll be back. We'll dine you and wine you at Maxim's and buy you the most beautiful frock in Paris.' Some of them did return after the war. Some of them returned every year, together with their wives and grown-up sons. And they came to the Folies-Bergère to see Lydia dance again. But then they sat in the best seats Lydia could find for them in the theatre. And as she danced, they pointed at her and told their wives: 'See that girl? Well, if it wasn't for her, I wouldn't be here with you now. She saved my life during the war.'

CHAPTER SIX:

THE CAT CATCHES THE CHICK

The winter of 1941 was the coldest anyone in Paris could remember, but in fact it was no colder than any other Parisian winter. But there was no coal, winter overcoats looked shabbier than usual and men put pieces of newspaper inside their shoes to plug the holes in their soles. Lydia shivered while she worked, forging documents. For business in the Lipski household continued as usual.

It took several agents to carry out the task of transporting messages and plans to British Intelligence. A man called Lucien R. normally fetched the plans from 'F 1'. Lipski's task for that particular case was then completed. But Lucien had to hand over the plans to another agent who would, in turn, hand it to another and so on until, eventually, the document would reach the hands of the 'master spy' and was transferred to England. The agent to whom Lucien handed his package was a young woman, a woman widely respected as one of the Resistance Movement's most trusted workers and a highly respected spy, certainly one of the most remarkable double-agents of WW2. Her name was Mathilde Carré and her code name in the Resistance was La Chatte, the Cat.* She was a brunette with hair in a spaced-out fringe along her forehead — the latest fashion of the day. Mathilde had high cheekbones and was certainly attractive. She might have been more than that, had she not tended towards plumpness, for she was of small stature into the bargain.

---

* See Appendix 3 for a more detailed account of The Cat

On the evening of November 20, 1941, Mathilde Carré paid a visit to the Lipskis. It was after this visit that the Cat became known as one of the cleverest double-agents in the history of counter-espionage, working at one and the same time for the Germans and the British. It was the Cat that caught the Chick.

While Lydia and her father ate their meagre supper of potato soup and bread, there was a loud knocking at their door.

'Who on earth?' Lipski's spoon halted half-way to his lips. Lydia stopped breathing for a split second and watched her father turning pale.

'Were you expecting anyone tonight, Papa?' she asked, frightened to see him so nervous.

'No,' he replied quietly. 'That knock. I don't like it. I don't like it one little bit.' He looked around him giving each inch of the room a detailed scrutiny. There was nothing lying around that might be of interest to the Germans — if it was the Germans. But before he could think further the knocking was repeated. 'Well, I'd — I'd better see who it is. Don't be afraid my little Cipinka, don't be afraid.' He moved towards the door slowly as though he was about to approach a bomb that was likely at any moment to explode.

'Who — who is it?' he asked, trying to make his voice sound as steady as possible.

'Ça va. It's only me, Micheline. I've come for the letters.' The girl's voice sounded cheerful, reassuring, through the door. But Lipski was still suspicious. In fact, he was more suspicious than ever. The 'letters' referred to the plans. Only two days previous, Lucien had collected the 'mail' and he was not due for another batch for almost a whole week. But apart from that, Micheline Carré had never visited the Movement headquarters personally. Lipski turned and looked at Lydia and Lydia saw her father wrestling with his thoughts. He rubbed the lobe of his right ear with thumb and forefinger — a habit of his whenever he felt nervous or uncertain of anything.

'All right,' he called at last. 'I'm just coming Micheline — but I don't know what letters you're talking about.'

Having made his decision Wladimir de Lipski acted quickly. He unbolted and opened the door in one movement. There stood the Cat, smiling a Mona Lisa sort of smile and greeting Lipski like some long lost brother, even though she had only seen him fleetingly once before during a meeting of section heads. She had never seen Lydia before and threw the girl a wave and a hello. 'Your daughter. Fine girl. Beautiful child.' Micheline Carré threw out the compliments haphazardly as though she was handing out pennies to a queue of beggars.

Only after the woman had entered the room could the shadow of another person be made out on the staircase outside. The shadow moved forward and developed into a man. He was wearing a brown raincoat. A grey felt hat was pulled slightly down over his eyes. He was thin and unsmiling. There was in his face a mixture of disgust and pity. If he liked his job he did not betray it then. He entered the room and looked around slowly, methodically, tasting every corner with his eyes. The silence seemed eternal.

It was Lipski who first spoke. 'Well, Micheline, aren't you going to introduce us to your friend? Won't you come in and sit down, Monsieur? We were just finishing supper. Perhaps you'll take a little something with us?' The thin man made no reply. He just looked strangely and silently at his would-be host, looked straight through him as a zombie might have done or a drug addict who had just taken a shot.

Micheline obliged. 'Of course, how silly of me. I'm sorry. This is Monsieur — Hugo Bleicher. Hugo, that's him,' and she pointed at Lipski, 'he's the leader of the outfit. And the girl, that's his daughter. She's the artist in the family.' The smile remained on her lips throughout. She was enjoying this dramatic exposé immensely. Yes, she was enjoying it all right.

In her smile was unhidden triumph. The smile spoke again: 'You thought you were all so very clever, didn't you? Well, you weren't. Not clever at all.' The smile hissed the words with the venom of a poisonous snake.

Bleicher,* took two slow steps towards Lipski, now standing with one hand on the table to support himself, pale and trembling more with anger than with fear. Bleicher, hands in pockets, and poker faced, said: 'It's no use trying to make a run for it. The house is surrounded. You might just as well come along quietly.' He spoke perfect French without a trace of an accent.

The Cat devoured Lydia with a stare and Lydia returned the look. She looked at the Cat with every ounce of hatred she could muster. And it was the Chick that out-stared the Cat. Micheline Carré was jealous of this beautiful young girl, jealous of her youth, jealous of her courage. 'Let's go,' she said and turned her back on the prisoners.

Outside it was cold and a thin drizzle fell over Paris. The streets were empty except for the Germans. All along the stairs of the apartment house stood heavily armed soldiers of the Wehrmacht. In front of the house and at each corner of the street were armoured trucks filled with more soldiers. The Germans had prepared themselves for a major operation.

Two *Panniers à Salade* (Black Marias) were drawn up on the opposite

---

*See Appendix 3 for more details about Hugo Bleicher,

side of the road. The Cat had obviously made a mistake. She had expected the Lipski flat to be filled with agents, had hoped to present the Germans with a bumper prize but, instead had found only a father and his daughter at their evening meal. The Germans who ransacked the apartment found very little — but nevertheless found sufficient evidence to bring a charge of espionage against the girl and the man. A few bottles of indian ink, some pens and the beginnings of two rice-paper plans of German camps outside Paris were discovered. Everything else — guns, ammunition, forged papers, cameras and printing presses — was in Mademoiselle Bertheaux's cellars. These, the methodical Germans had overlooked. That hiding place was never found and remained undisturbed until after the war.

The trucks and soldiers had arrived on the scene silently, so silently that neither Lydia nor her father had heard even the banging of a door. Now, however, they screeched away with all the noise of launching rockets. Sirens wailed, horns hooted, wheels screamed round corners as the long convoy bearing two pathetic prisoners careered its way to the Hotel Edward VII which had been taken over by the Sicherheitspolizei (German Security Police). Lydia and her father were roughly pushed out of their truck by eight hands while other German soldiers stood in front and behind pointing sub-machine guns and pistols at their heads.

'*Schnell! Macht schnell! Los, Mensch, los!*' The orders were hurled at Lipski and Lydia as they were pushed through the swing doors and into the brightly lit foyer of the hotel. Orders telling them to hurry continued to be shouted as they stumbled along the thick red carpet and up the stairs to the first floor. Other uniformed men took over from the soldiers and pushed them roughly into a small room. The room was in darkness, smelled musty. The door was locked.

'Oh, Papa, Papa, what are we to do?' sobbed Lydia, falling into her father's arms and weeping hot tears onto his shoulders. She had not cried until this moment. For until now, she had shown only defiance, hatred and bravery in her face. The strain had worn off and she now felt terribly, terribly tired and frightened. Her father pulled her close to him and whispered into her ear: 'Shsh, darling, be quiet. Don't say anything. This room is probably wired and everything is being recorded. So say nothing. Later on you'll be asked a lot of questions. Remember, my darling, you know nothing, nothing at all. Do you understand?' He was whispering very close to Lydia's ear and the girl nodded agreement. 'You know nothing and you must deny every charge they make against you. They may threaten to kill me — they may even tell you they have already killed me but don't let them fool you, whatever they say.

Right?' Lydia nodded but wept more bitterly than ever.

He continued aloud: 'Don't worry, my darling. Don't cry. We'll be out of here soon. After all, the Germans would not harm innocent people, would they? There's been some mistake. Some terrible mistake. I can't understand what all this is about but it won't be long before all is explained and we'll be able to go home again. Who was that woman who came to us tonight? Have you ever seen her before?'

'No,' sobbed Lydia, playing up to her father, and added truthfully: 'I never saw her before in my life. What did she mean by calling me the artist in the family and you the leader?'

'Maybe she saw you dancing in Pigalle, sweetheart. After all, that's artistic what you do. Certainly the Germans have always appreciated your dancing up to now, haven't they? It's all just a ghastly mistake..'

Before he could say any more, the door was opened and a German in the hated uniform of the Gestapo stood silhouetted in the corridor light. 'Lipski Come along,' he ordered. 'You'd better say good-bye to your little girl. You won't be seeing each other again, I'll take bets on that.' He laughed menacingly. Lipski took Lydia's head between his hands and looked her in the eyes. 'There must be some mistake, Lydia darling, and I'll find out at once what it is and get us released. You won't forget what I said. Don't worry and everything will be all right.'

Lydia sobbed loudly. 'Don't leave me, Papa, don't go. Please, please don't go. I love you so much.'

During the sixteen years he had had Lydia, her father could only remember two occasions when Lydia had told him she loved him — and on both of them the confession was made in the same way that all children make it. 'Whom do you love more, Lydia, your Daddy or your Mummy?' someone would ask at a tea party. 'I love them both the same,' the child would answer obediently. 'Yes, but which one do you love that little bit more,' the visitor would persist. 'Papa,' Lydia would answer shyly and the rest of the family would laugh and pour out more coffee and hand round the home baked cakes. The other occasion was when Lipski tried to send Lydia away, out of France, away from the oncoming German invaders. She used her love for him as one of her reasons for staying. He had then taken it as it was meant — an excuse and an additional argument for him not to send her away. Apart from those two times, Wladimir de Lipski could not remember hearing his daughter say she loved him.

Now her cry tore at his heart. He wanted to take her into his arms and hold her just as he had used to do when she was small and had come running into the house crying because she had fallen and cut her knee or because some boys had hit her. Then he would pick her up and cradle her gently. 'It's all right... shsh... Papa is here... it's all right,' he'd say. And soon the crying would stop and Lydia would be her old romping, cheerful self again. But this time he could not pick her up, could not kiss her and hold her. He tried to say a word of comfort to her but found that the words just would not come. The lump in his throat was choking him and, as he turned his face to the light filtering through into the room, the German officer saw tears streaming down an old man's cheeks. 'Come along, hurry up. We've not got all day.' The door closed. The light was gone. And Lydia was alone with the dark.

She sank to the ground, weak, exhausted with weeping and with fear. A sudden loneliness swept over her, enveloped her, held her with so tight a grip that the tears dried cold upon her face. She shivered and suddenly realized that she was wearing only a thin dress. They had not allowed her to pack anything, had not even let her take an overcoat. The realization that all was over came to her now: she would dance no more to the cheers of Germans and French and Poles and Englishmen, would no longer be able to help end the war. The Germans have won and all is over. I shall never again see my father or my mother or even my brother, she thought and the horror was imprinted upon the darkness and the walls that she could not see seemed only to echo her thoughts. In the silence she stopped and listened to a fast, irregular beating and suddenly realized it was her heart.

Lydia half rose to her knees. There was only one thing left to do and she did it. She prayed half silently, half aloud with a sincerity she had never before shown in her prayers.

'Oh, Holy Mary, Mother of God, please, please, save my father. Don't let them hurt him. If we have done wrong, sweet Jesus, then forgive us our sins. We only did what we thought to be right. Honestly, we were only doing what any honest French citizen would do. And please, God, please give me the strength to survive what is in store for me. Let me not tell them anything. Let me not weaken and deceive those who are still working for France. Let me not mention their names, dear God. But, above all, dearest Jesus, save my father. Save him for me and for my mother's sake. Bless him and all of us and those who are doing what they consider is just and good. I know not for what I have fought but I know that what I did was not wrong, could not have been wrong, for even the priest at church told us that with your help, dear Jesus, France would be saved from the Germans who have come and taken away our liberty, our happiness and our joy to live and love. Dearest God, I have never before asked You for anything sensible. Well, I'm asking You now. Please forgive us and give us strength. Come to us now, dear Jesus and take us into Your arms. Amen.'

Lydia continued to kneel and pray for many minutes more, repeating the same prayer, the same wishes again and again until, in the silence of her prayers, she fell asleep.

She was stretched out on the cold, hard stone floor, still sleeping soundly when the door opened. 'On your feet quick! Come along, you little bitch, we've not got all day. This isn't a holiday camp. Come on.' It was the same Gestapo officer who had come for her father. Lydia opened her eyes and rubbed them. For a moment she had no idea where she was or who this strangely dressed man was. She had not slept so well for many a night even though now her bones ached and her whole body felt stiff and cold. Slowly her memory returned to her. She looked round for her father, but he was not there. She was alone and the room was dimly alight. It was dawn. As she regained consciousness completely, she made out the rain against the window pane. She looked in the direction of the window. It was high up in the room. The light was pressing through it and she could see that there were steel bars on the other side of the glass. She looked again at the man in the door. He looked haggard and worn out. His chin was covered with an unshaven shadow. He looked as though he had not been to bed all night.

The German grew impatient. With two steps he was at her side. 'Get up, I said. Don't you understand French, you little whore?' He emphasized his command with a sharp kick from his boot It caught Lydia in the hip and she gave a little cry as the pain shot through her body. She slowly, painfully rose to her feet. 'Come on, move !' shouted the German and pushed her so roughly that she stumbled through the door and fell headlong onto the carpet in the corridor. The man was at her side again and pulled her up by her shoulder and, half pushing, half supporting her, marched her along the passage to another door. This he opened and steered Lydia through.

This time she found herself in a large, well furnished room with a beautiful chandelier of many coloured crystals throwing bright light over excellent Louis XV chairs, a table, a settee, and a large mahogany desk.

Behind this sat a small man with close-cropped hair and heavily-rimmed, thick-lensed glasses. He smiled at Lydia and beckoned her to sit down in the comfortable chair in front of the desk. She did so, never taking her eyes off the man. For a long time he said nothing but merely tapped a pencil on his knuckles and looked at the young girl in front of him. There was no cruelty in the look, no threats. It was just an empty, vacant look that seemed to pierce through Lydia's thin dress and made her feel uncomfortable without making her feel afraid. At last he spoke and his voice was soothing, deep, almost melodious.

'What is your name, child?' he said and sounded like the priest at her local church. He spoke reasonably good French and pronounced each word slowly and carefully in order to hide his teutonic accent.

'Lydia, sir. Lydia de Korczak Lipski.'

'Ah, yes. You are Polish, are you not? The daughter of Prince de Korczak Lipski?'

'Yes. Yes, sir.'

'Yes, of course. Well, I had the honour of meeting and speaking with your father, the Prince, last night. We had a nice long chat together. He was extremely helpful. A charming man. You must indeed be very proud to be the daughter of so good a father, eh?'

'Why, yes, sir, I am.' Lydia was beginning to like this kind little man with the thick glasses. How nice it was of him, she thought, to be so complimentary about her father. Maybe he had already been released and was waiting at home for her. She ventured the question. 'Where is my father, sir? Could I go and see him please?'

'Certainly you may soon, very soon. Have you eaten breakfast yet?'

'No — er — not yet, but I…'

'Then you must have some with me.' He looked up at the officer who had brought Lydia in. 'Bring us a large pot of coffee and some croissants, Hoffmann — with butter.'

Butter! Lydia had not eaten butter for a long time. She had almost forgotten what it tasted like. Dry bread had been the main fare at her home since the war came to France and the few ounces of margarine did not go very far. Hoffmann left the room and the little man rose from his chair and went to the window. He looked out and muttered: 'Tut-tut, raining again. Does it always rain in Paris? I thought that only the sun shone here and that everything was gay and full of life.'

'It used to be like that, sir.' Lydia forgot herself.

'Used to be, Lydia? What do you mean? When did it used to be like that?'

'Well, sir, I meant that — well, it used to be like that in the summer and it will be like that again soon — er — when the spring comes.'

'Ah yes, the spring. *Im wundervollen Monat Mai.* Or did you mean that it used to be like that before the war, eh? That's what you meant, wasn't it? Go on, you can tell me. We're quite alone.'

'Well, yes. It was wonderful in Paris before the war. Were you ever here, sir, before the war, I mean?'

'No Lydia, I've never been to Paris before. This is my first time. And I hope that when the war is over I shall be able to come again and see it as you remember it. I don't like the war, do you? Nasty business, war.'

He turned from the window and faced Lydia, looking at her long and hard. 'I've got a little girl just like you at home, you know? Her hair is blonde too, just like yours. So you see, I don't want this war to go on any longer than you do. But it won't last much longer. When Germany has won, we shall all be able to go home to our families and live happily for the rest of our lives.'

Lydia found this little man who had a daughter just like her, most 'sympathique'. She felt she could talk to him just as she could to her own father. Maybe, she thought, her prayers had been answered. She felt encouraged sufficiently to ask: 'But what if Germany does not win the war, sir?' What if the other side wins?'

The man returned to his desk and sat down. He picked up his pencil and began knocking it against the knuckles of his other hand again. After a while he said: 'I don't believe that is possible, Lydia. You see, we Germans have much greater strength than the British and the Russians put together. The English were not prepared, you see. They had nothing when the war started and they still have nothing. As for the Russians — well, they have a lot of men but those men don't know how to fight battles. Apart from that, we are fighting for an ideal. We want to make this a better world to live in for everyone — and particularly for young people like you, Lydia.'

The door opened and Hoffmann came back carrying a tray filled with a pot of steaming coffee, a plate full of croissants and a dish of butter, cups, saucers, plates and knives. He placed the tray down on the desk and poured out the coffee. It smelled good. Very good. It was a smell Lydia loved. It reminded her of the breakfasts her mother used to make. It was the smell to which she awoke in the mornings — those sunny mornings when Paris was alive. Hoffmann, big burly Hoffmann who had treated her so brutally only a few minutes before, whose kick she could still feel on her hip, now handed her a cup of coffee and a plate with two warm croissants. The little man behind the desk was already spreading butter on one of his croissants and took a large bite out of it. Lydia sipped her coffee. It was good, excellent coffee and she felt the warmth returning to her body as she swallowed it.

'That is why, Lydia,' continued the little man, 'we feel a little hurt when some French people — people whom we would like to call our friends and brothers — do silly things to hinder us in winning the war more quickly. Had it not been for some of these very strange actions, the war may have been over weeks ago. Oh, yes. I'm not exaggerating. Weeks ago. Then we would have gone back to Germany and left France to lead the same sort of life she was leading before — before we came. Now as I said before oh, Hoffmann, fill up the young lady's cup, there's a good chap.' He waited till his order had been carried out.

'Now as I was saying before, Lydia, your father and I had a nice long, cosy chat — just like we are having now. We had dinner together, didn't we Hoffmann? (Hoffmann nodded and said. '*Jawohl, Herr Oberst,* '). And your father, such a good man that, agreed with me that it would be far better to come to a reasonable understanding. He told us all about what he and you were doing but, of course, said that he had no idea that he or you were doing wrong. You see, he had never met any real Germans at all and didn't realize that we were — well, not quite such nasty, selfish people as we were made out to be by British propaganda. Propaganda is a very natural weapon in war, of course, and a very harmful one. Since your father had only the word of propaganda to go by, he believed it and thought we were all out to kill every Frenchman in France. Ha-ha-ha, a very silly though understandable thought in the circumstances, eh? After our friendly chat, however, he realized his grave mistake and over a good glass of your excellent French Cognac and a real Havana cigar, we came to a clear understanding. I hope you will be equally as sensible as he was, Lydia, my dear, and then we can all go home and get some sleep. Now, what do you say?'

Lydia finished her second cup of coffee. She had listened to every word as attentively as though she was at school and was being examined in her most difficult subject. This time she found the answer easily.

'What was it, sir, this understanding you came to with Papa?'

'Quite simply this, Lydia. In return for his freedom — you'll understand, of course, that we had to arrest him after the information we received from one of his own agents — in return for us letting him go back home.'

'So Papa is at home Oh, how wonderful, oh thank you, sir. You are really most kind.' Lydia felt like embracing this little man with the slow, mellow voice.

'Yes, child, he's back at home and waiting for you. Anyway, before he left me, he told me the names of the others in the Movement he was leading.'

Lydia's heart missed a beat. She could not believe her ears. This, surely this was untrue. Her father would never do such a thing, not even for the largest glass of Cognac in the world and the biggest Havana cigar — not her father. What was it he had told her? 'You know nothing and you must deny any charge they make against you.' He would not, immediately after saying that, go and tell the Germans the names of all the agents who belonged to 'F 1'. Surely the little man was bluffing.

'Now I don't think we need detain you much more, Lydia. 'You can go and join your father very soon. All we want you to do is to tell us everything you know about your father's little Movement and where he hides the guns and ammunition and the names of those who work for him. Now that's not very difficult, is it?'

Lydia thought rapidly. What did all this mean? Here was a man being nice, actually nice to her, giving her a good breakfast the like of which she had not tasted in well over a year and telling her that her father was a nice man — and a traitor.

'But, sir, if my father has already told you all these things — and I really cannot understand why he should tell you things that are not true as he has not been leading anything like you say and has no guns anywhere — then why should you wish me to tell you similar things that are not true? I really cannot tell you about guns and names of people who have been in the Movement because I simply don't know what you're talking about.'

The pencil began rapping knuckles again and the eyes behind the thick lenses grew impatient. 'Now Lydia, don't be silly. You're behaving like a child and I thought of you as a grown young woman with a lot of sense just like your father. If you don't tell us what I have just asked you, I shall find no alternative but to keep you here until you do tell us. Then your father will get very worried sitting all alone at home waiting for you. Now come along. Have another cup of coffee — Hoffmann, pour another cup — and then tell me all you know.'

'I'm really sorry, Monsieur. I wish I could tell you the things you wish to know, but really and truly I have no idea what to tell you. How can I tell you things I don't know? I could not tell you any lies, could I?'

'*Zum donnerwetter nochmal*, you are lying now, you stupid, wicked girl!' The little man had jumped up from his desk and crashed his fist down on it. His face had suddenly turned red with rage. He screamed: 'The names of all the people who worked for your father. Quick. Quick. Tell me!'

Lydia remained silent and put the cup to her lips to drink the coffee. The little man had jumped to her side and with a sweep of his hand had knocked the cup away. The hot coffee ran down Lydia's dress and burned through to her skin. 'Ow,' Lydia cried and jumped up from her chair. 'The coffee. Look, you've spilled it all down my frock.'

Her protest was met with a resounding slap across the face and she was knocked back into the chair. 'I shall do more to you than merely spill a few drops of coffee on your dress if you don't tell me those names.'

'But I've just told you. I don't know any names. Oh, please let me go home to my father. Please!'

Another slap from the German's hand hit her other cheek. Lydia began to cry. 'Why won't you believe me,' she sobbed. 'I don't know any names. I — don't — know — anything.'

'Hoffmann, you'd better see if you can get any sense out of the little vixen.' The little man, completely exasperated, turned his back on Lydia and returned to the window. He was breathing heavily and pulled out a large white handkerchief with which he mopped his brow and hands.

'Jawohl, sofort Herr Oberst.' There was a tone of pleasure and gratitude in Hoffmann's voice. He came and sat himself at the edge of his chief's desk facing Lydia. 'You heard, didn't you? I shall get those names out of you if anyone will, so you'd better tell me them now before you regret it. And I can assure you (he bent down low towards Lydia) you will regret it if you don't give me those names quickly. You remember that little kick I gave you back in your room? Well, there's a lot more where that came from. I know various tricks for little girls like you.'

Hoffmann took out a packet of cigarettes and lit himself one. He blew the smoke into Lydia's face. 'Are you ready to talk?'

'I — I have already told the other Monsieur all I know.' Hoffmann did not bother to wait for a better cue. He lashed out at Lydia, landing two neat, stinging slaps across her face with the back of his hand. Lydia sobbed with the pain.

'What are the names of the men who worked for your father?'

'I don't know what you're talking about.' More slaps. Harder this time.

'Where does your father keep the arms and ammunition?'

'What arms and... ?' Further slaps. Lydia was beginning to feel faint. Some blood fell from the corner of her mouth and mixed with the coffee stains on her dress.

'I'll give you just one more chance to tell me the names and where those guns are hidden. If you don't tell me (Hoffmann's face was close to Lydia's and she could smell his breath. It smelled of bad drains and through the tears she saw his teeth. They were brown and broken.) — if you don't tell me, then I shall hurt you really badly. Now where...'

'I don't know... I don't know... I don't know,' shouted Lydia, closing her eyes tightly and shaking her head violently. 'I don't know....'

Then she screamed. It was a scream that filled the room and bounced off the mirrors on the walls. It flew round and round, that scream, round and round the room. And the room flew round and round with it until all light disappeared and Lydia found herself swimming through a dark vacuum into nothingness. She fainted.

For Hoffmann had just pressed out the burning cigarette on her neck.

CHAPTER SEVEN:

PRISON, TORTURES AND NIGHTMARES

The cell at the Santé prison was damp, dark and cold. Santé means health in French. With the possible exception of the Sweet Water Canal in Egypt, there cannot exist a greater misnomer than La Santé. Whatever it was, it was certainly not healthy and prisoners usually ended up in a hospital for lengthy stretches after having paid for their crimes in this Paris prison. Lydia's thin dress clung to her body soaked by the moisture streaming from the bare walls and by the sweat of fear and fever. After her first taste of torture at the hands of the *Sicherheitspolizei* she had been thrown bodily into the back of a French Black Maria and driven through the night to the prison. Once there, she was photographed from all angles, was given a rapid and by no means thorough medical examination and was 'de-loused' even though she had never even seen either flea or louse. Strong wardresses pushed her along narrow, lifeless corridors, up steel staircases and into the cell. The door slammed shut and the sound re-echoed emptily along the passages. Bolts were thrown across the door and a key turned in the lock. Then the steps of the wardresses retreated noisily until all was silence — all except for the sound of sleeping bodies in other cells. Lydia strained her ears. Every muscle in her body was awake, tensed and expectant.

She listened for the living, listened to every little snore, every sigh, every movement of a body turning in its sleep. She did not know where the sounds were coming from, did not know who was making them. Somewhere a woman screamed in her sleep. It was a scream that brought Lydia to her feet. She wanted to scream too. She wanted the whole world to scream. But all she could do was to sob quietly to herself. The scream was repeated and from along the corridor somewhere, Lydia heard a woman's voice shouting: *'Oh, ça va, merde alors*, let's get some sleep, for Christ's sake.' And all was silent again. And suddenly Lydia realized that she was alone.

The realization came to her with a shock. The sounds from the sleepers had disappeared as her ears became accustomed to them and now she could hear nothing except a dreadful silence. The silence seemed to close in on her, enfold her in its black cloak. She felt suffocated by the silence. Suffocated. Then she screamed. She screamed as she had never before screamed in her life. She put every ounce of energy into that scream, letting her lungs breathe in the damp, stale air that smelled of crumbling stone and urine, and explode with a piercing, high-pitched screech that split the silence and tore through the walls. She sucked in the air for a second time and produced another scream that kept company to the first and both screams soared round and round the cell, through the walls and the door and around the prison into freedom.

She wanted to follow them out and stumbled in the darkness towards the door, pounding it with her fists, wanting to break it down. 'Let me out! Let me out of here! For God's sake let me out! Why am I here? Why do you leave me in the dark? Let me out! Let me out, I say!' Her voice was no longer her own. It was a screech, a yell, the noise made by a trapped foal on the bleak moors. And soon her voice was joined by others. No one told her to be quiet. No one ordered her to go back to sleep. Those whom she had awakened realized that here was a new prisoner. Fists, hundreds of fists, pounded their locked doors as though the doors were jungle drums. And soon the beating grew rhythmical and slow. Thump — thump — thump — thump — thump — thump. Now voices reached her across the pounding fists. 'Welcome so Sing-Sing, *chérie*…' Don't let the bastards get you down.' 'What are you in for? Black marketeering?' 'Make yourself at home, Dearie, for they'll never let you see your home again.' 'Murder? Did you murder a *boche*? I'd wipe out the whole lot of 'em if I had the chance.' 'Don't let them get you down, les cons. Lydia swam in the noise, her own screams drowned in the depths of the other prisoners' shouts. She wanted to answer their questions, wanted to shake their hands, wanted to be with them. But no one seemed to want an answer from her. The questions were thrown to her in rapid succession and the pounding fists continued to beat out a rhythm on the doors.

Somewhere in the distance, a girl began to sing. 'Allons enfants….' The pounding fists stopped hammering and, instead, full throated voices joined in.

'Allons enfants de la pa—tri—e
Le jour de gloire est a—rri—vé..

But the Marseillaise was interrupted. Feet were running along the corridors and lights were thrown on. 'Quiet! Silence the lot of you! Will you be quiet, you bitches!' Wardresses shouted the orders and the grill on Lydia's door flew open. A face peered in at her. 'I suppose this is your doing, you little swine,' the voice that belonged to the face yelled. 'If I get so much as one little peep out of you again tonight, I'll have you whipped. Is that understood? Now get down and go to sleep. You'll need it.' The grill banged shut. The feet retreated once more accompanied by undertone mutterings and curses. One or two of the braver prisoners shouted comments at the wardress. 'Go shag yourselves, you ugly bitches you.' 'Traitors... Assassins...' 'Go back and sleep with your filthy *boches*... They're the only ones who'd sleep with you...' *'Emmerdeurs... Filles du diable...'*

The lights went out and all was dark again. And, little by little, silence returned to the prison. Soon all Lydia could hear was the snores she had heard before and the bodies moving in their sleep.

While the light had been on, Lydia was able to look at her cell. It was bare, except for a sack of straw that had holes in it, a tin basin and a tin jug in one corner and a second tin basin with a piece of wood over the top of it which was to serve her natural needs in another corner. The walls glistened with the damp perspiration. When it was again dark, she could not remember seeing a window and although she strained her eyes searching for an opening, she could not find it.

But in the darkness and the silence she realized that she had friends, that there were others in the prison who felt just like she did, that they, too, were lonely and afraid. Still weeping quietly to herself and feeling very, very cold, she felt her way to the thing they called a bed and sank down on it. She closed her eyes and slowly, agonizingly slowly, sleep came upon her. Only her subconscious was still awake and took her into the world of dreams.

Her father entered the cell and the joy of seeing him made her leap up from the damp straw. He beckoned her to follow him and she did, skipping along the corridor of the prison like a gazelle. Her father moved quickly down the long staircase, taking two, three steps at a time. At every landing he stopped, turned his face to Lydia and beckoned silently. She ran as fast as she could but her legs felt heavy and weak and the staircase was interminably long. When would they reach the bottom? Her father disappeared round a corner and stood at the big gate that led to the street and liberty.

Strange, thought Lydia, that there are no guards, no wardresses, not even the big, fat one who had pushed her into her cell only a little while ago. The gate opened and her father beckoned to her to hurry. He opened the gate a little further and ran out into the street. Lydia also reached the doorway now and she saw that it was light outside. The sun seemed to be shining behind dawn's early clouds. It would be a beautiful day. A beautiful day. She saw that there were already people about. Nobody seemed to see her, or, if they did, they were not taking any notice of her. Oh, it was great to be free again. Then she heard a shout. 'Lipski. Lipski, come back.' She searched the crowd of people for the man who had shouted. Then she saw him. It was the little man who had been so kind to her at first during her interrogation and who had then had her tortured. She wanted to shout to her father to be careful but it was too late. The man had caught up with him, had held onto his shoulder. His assistant Hoffmann was there too. The people in the street had suddenly disappeared, probably afraid for their own lives, and Lydia stopped in her tracks. The Germans were now tying her poor father's hands behind his back. Hoffmann threw a rope over the lower branch of a tree. To Lydia's horror, she saw that it was not a tree but a scaffold. How stupid of her to think it was a tree. Her father was standing on a scaffold and, good God in Heaven, they were going to hang him. The rope was round his neck and Hoffmann was awaiting his orders.

Lydia looked at her father, her poor father, looking so thin, so pale. She had never seen him looking quite so thin and white. With his hands tied and the rope around his neck, he looked so pathetic. Lipski caught his daughter's eyes and shrugged his shoulders. *'C'est fini, Cipinka,'* he whispered and he smiled a sad little smile. Lydia had to stop then. This was murder. They were murdering her father. She ran towards him but after she had taken only a few steps, she felt hands holding her back. The hands were cold and their grip was like steel. She could not move. She turned round to see who was holding her. And she stared straight into the face of Micheline Carré. The little woman sneered at her. 'Cipinka—pah.' She spat the name and then she laughed and she looked down into Lydia's face and Lydia saw that it was no longer Micheline Carré that was holding her, but a Gestapo officer and his face was not a face but a skull, a dead, ugly, bony skull.... And Lydia screamed.

Lydia screamed and awoke screaming, her body bathed in sweat. She was not out in the street but lying on the cold, hard floor of her dark cell. She stifled her scream and sobbed as she groped her way back to the straw mattress. She could not recall ever having had so vivid a dream. It was a nightmare that was to return to her time and again during the first few weeks of her prison life. Always she saw her father being hanged by Germans from a scaffold and sometimes the scaffold would be flying the Nazi swastika flag. It is a nightmare she was never to forget.

For two interminable days she lay in her cell undisturbed except for the pounding of her heart and a gnawing in her stomach. No wardress came to see her. No food, no drink was handed her. Lydia was left completely on her own, hungry, miserable, cold. Only a tiny window threw some light down upon her and she could see the clouds that were her only friends during the days. To keep herself from losing her mind, she would lie on her bed of straw, her head resting on her arms and look up at those specks of clouds, counting them as they passed, making bets with imaginary spirits in the cell how long it would take for one cloud to pass and for a patch of blue sky to appear. 'I bet you,' she addressed the wall on her right, 'that that cloud will have gone by the time I have counted exactly sixty-six... one — two — three — four...' Sometimes the cloud would pass by the time she had reached a mere twenty-five and she would lose the bet. 'That's 300 francs I owe you and 350 you owe me, so that makes me 50 francs better off than you.'

At other moments she would compose menus of the most delicious meals she was going to make for herself and her father the moment she was released from this prison. 'Now, let's see, we'll start off with a delicious Bortsch of lots and lots of beef stock, beetroots, lemon juice and a great mass of sour cream. After that we'll have some delicious filets of sole a la Normande, cooked in white wine and garnished with croutons fried in butter and prawns.

'Ah, and then how about a good old boeuf strogonoff with mushrooms and cream? Yes, I think a boeuf strogonoff would go down very well. Then there'd be the cheeses of course—a nice and ripe Camembert or Brie or even a Petit Suisse with sugar or even strawberries... Then we could have some fresh fruit — a banana and a juicy apple — and a nice creamy gateau with nuts on top of it and cups and cups of hot steaming coffee — black of course.

Lydia's mouth would water at the thought of all these delicacies, most of which were only vague memories of days past when her mother made certain specialties when visitors came to the house. She would be allowed to stay up later than usual on those occasions and watch her father blow satisfied smoke rings from his after-dinner cigar and smack his lips after tasting his *digestif.* Her dream would end after hearing some distractive noise coming from another cell or from the street below and she would again stare at the clouds and the bare walls. Had a rat made an appearance at this stage in her cell, she would have welcomed it. Her loneliness was overpowering and her hunger grew to a painful strength in her continually gurgling stomach. How long, she thought, would they keep her here without so much as a bite of bread? Maybe, she thought with an ever growing terror, they had forgotten all about her, had forgotten that she was in this damp cell, and were never going to come and open the door to her. The thought of death did not frighten Lydia so much as the thought of a death in loneliness, a death from starvation.

Not even a close examination of her cell could keep this thought at bay. Under the dampness, the constantly trickling dampness of the walls, she was able to make out scratched messages or names. Most of them were the sort of crude wordings written by frustrated, sex-starved people upon the walls of public lavatories. But then, this was, after all, no more than a public lavatory. The cell stank of urine and excrement. It had not been cleaned for years it seemed, and if it had been cleaned, no amount of scrubbing would rid it of that stench. The monkey house at the zoo smelled better than this. 'Marie-Antoinette slept here,' read one message, 'and she was better off than Jeanne Porreau.' Who was Jeanne Porreau? thought Lydia. What could she have done to end up here? What did she look like? And she would stop and consider this Mademoiselle Porreau (or was it perhaps Potteau? Those r's were not very clear they might be t's), her height, colour of eyes, whether she was thin or fat (if she was in here, she was probably as thin as a skeleton), whether her hair was long or short, black or blonde. Lydia composed a picture of the woman in her mind, slowly, savouring each little detail for as long as possible. And what did this poor Jeanne do? What was her unspeakable crime? Lydia thought of everything that might have brought her here. The Resistance was always her first thought, for it was what she herself had experienced. But perhaps she had killed someone — her husband maybe, or a German… or maybe she had been a thief; now what could she have stolen?

This game could be kept up for hours on end, Lydia found. She had plenty of time, after all, and she took it. Why should she race over her little discoveries in the cell for who could tell how long she was to be kept there before she died?

The only thing in the cell that she wanted desperately to examine and examine quickly, she was unable to reach. The window was too high up and she jumped time and again but her outstretched hand would not reach it. It remained therefore, a mystery to her. She knew that the window was not too far from the street because she could hear cars passing from time to time and sometimes she even managed to make out the sound of men's voices bidding each other a cheerful good-morning or commenting loudly about the weather being so rotten and blaspheming it. But these snippets of distant conversation were all-too rare and even the cars seemed few and far between.

Lydia, surprised at her own logical deductions, surmised that the street below her window probably was one of the alleys at the rear of the prison and not one of the main boulevards in front of it. Oh, but how she wished she could see for herself.

The first two days seemed never to end and the nights dragged on and on. Lydia heard the warders pass by her cell, heard other prisoners shuffle silently past. On one occasion there was a gentle knock on her cell door and she rushed to it, expecting it to open. But there was nothing. Nothing. Nobody was coming in. It must have been one of the prisoners walking past who had knocked — just to let her know she had not been forgotten by her colleagues.

When she heard the wardresses going by, Lydia would rush to the door and call out or bang her fists against its hard wood. 'Hey, what about some food? I'm still here! Hey, have you forgotten me? Can't you hear? Oh, please let me out. Please, please, please. But her calls and bangings had no effect. The wardresses walked past. Only one called out to her to shut up or else she'd never get any food at all and would die and she couldn't care less if she died anyway. Lydia gave up trying to shout and bang her way out of the cell and merely listened to the footsteps of those unknowns beyond the door who were able to walk along the blissful corridors of a prison instead of seeing nothing but four ugly, ugly, ugly walls, those slimy walls. Lydia quenched, if that is the word, her thirst by running her finger along the walls, collecting up the dirty damp and then licking it off her finger. It tasted foul, but it was, at least, wet and helped relieve her parched throat.

And the nights… the nights were the most terrifying. Her body all aching, her nostrils filled with the dank, acrid stench, her eyes aching for sleep but her mind alert and afraid to allow sleep to come. Lydia pinched herself to keep awake, listened to the snoring of the others in surrounding cells. She dared not sleep. For she feared the nightmare of that first night, she feared to look death in the face again. When she eventually did fall asleep, her dreams saw to it that she did not sleep for long.

As the third day dawned, Lydia had given up all hope of ever seeing the outside world again. She was convinced that the Germans, if they had not forgotten about her, were leaving her to die, deliberately starving her to death. Even her stomach, tired of having none of its loud protests satisfied, had given up its rumblings. Now it just ached with emptiness instead. The warders made their usual rounds, opening other cell doors, shouting instructions to the prisoners to move themselves fast and that this was no damn holiday camp and similar expressions. Lydia could hear the prisoners yawning and cursing

— giving, in fact, all the usual reactions to being awakened at a ridiculous hour after a good night's sleep. Lydia rose, stretched herself, winced with the pain of her aching bones — it felt as though her ribs were going to explode through her skin — and walked slowly round and round the cell. This sort of exercise kept her from total collapse. Despite her hunger and her weakness, she walked as much as she possibly could during the day in order to keep her blood circulation going, and bring warmth to her body.

A key was introduced into her door. Her door. Lydia stopped, froze to the spot, hardly daring to breathe. She strained her ears but there was no need. The door was already open. A wardress stood in the cell. She was fat and huge and reminded Lydia at once of the Brunnhilde she had seen together with her father when he had taken her to the Opera for her first experience of Wagner. Here was Brunnhilde in person. Only she was French.

'Come with me, you,' Brunnhilde ordered. Lydia suddenly felt even weaker. She could feel her knees shaking as she stepped forward towards the woman in the doorway. Beyond her she could just make out the corridor and the rails of steel. Brunnhilde took hold of Lydia's arm firmly and led her quickly down the iron staircase, along more corridors and finally into a large, warm, oak-panelled room. The heat hit Lydia like a whip. Before her was a table with two telephones, a lot of papers, files and a desk calendar and three men. They were sitting behind the table, dressed in neat, dark suits. A fourth man, standing by the window, staring out through the bars, wore the uniform of an officer in the German Wehrmacht.

'Ah, Mademoiselle Lipski,' cooed one of the three civilians in perfect French. 'Sit down, won't you?' Lydia slowly sat down in the comfortable leather covered chair in front of the table. She realized suddenly how dirty she must be looking and instinctively put one hand up to her hair, tidying it as best she could. The men were staring at her and she felt their stares drilling through her thin body. The heat and the silence made her feel drowsy and she had to force her eyes open. In the background she heard the ticking of a clock. It seemed to come from behind her.

One of the three civilians offered Lydia a cigarette which she declined. 'I — I don't smoke, thank you,' she said and was surprised at her own voice.

It sounded hollow and hoarse. The crystal clear tones that used to be hers were gone, replaced by the more grating, metallic sound made by a person many years older.

The man in the middle of the three who were sitting down spoke next. He was older than the others and greying at the temples. He looked like a doctor or a priest. 'Mademoiselle, allow me to apologize for the discomfort you must have been suffering here. The prison is somewhat overcrowded and we are very short staffed, you realize. I am sorry we could not offer you better surroundings.'

The third man, whose head looked out of proportion with the rest of his body, from what she could see of it behind the table, then shot questions at her. The small mouth that opened above an almost chinless face and which seemed far removed from his narrow eyes that were sunk deep in his protruding forehead, exploded the first question.

'Perhaps, Mademoiselle, you would be good enough to tell us now the names of those who collaborated with you? Who are they? Where do they live? Let us have these few details and you may go home.'

Lydia's silence seemed to shock her inquisitors. They looked at each other in sullen amazement and then stared again at Lydia. The man sitting in the middle tut-tutted for a while and then said, almost kindly:

'Mademoiselle Lipski, I don't think you realize that we wish you no harm. It is not our habit to ill-treat girls of your age. You must understand that. Now what I am going to tell you may come as a severe shock to you and I am deeply sorry to have to be the one to have to break such tidings to you. Your father, Mademoiselle, is dead. He was shot yesterday afternoon. He was sentenced the day before as a spy and executed.'

Lydia's eyes grew wide. Her body shook. She was shivering despite the heat in that room. 'No no, you're lying. You're lying,' she whispered, but when she looked up at the men again, it seemed as though their faces were not human at all but were skulls. They were the same skulls she had seen in her nightmares. In her heart she felt they were telling her the truth. The man in uniform turned from the window. As though from a great distance, his voice floated to her.

'*Ein Mann Namens Lucien R.* (Full surname withheld by request of Lucien's surviving family.) *ist auch erschossen worden…*' he said in German and turned back to the window.

The third inquisitor translated. 'A man by the name of Rxxx —Lucien Rxxx—has also been shot. In fact, Mademoiselle, we have been fortunate enough to arrest every member of your organization. Most of them are dead, I'm sorry to have to inform you. All will be dead soon.'

They were all looking at her again, expecting her to speak, but Lydia remained silent. Her eyes felt as though they would burst and she swallowed back the tears she wanted so desperately to shed. All she could think of was her father, her poor, dead father. She crossed herself, closed her eyes and folded her hands to pray for his soul. Her action so embarrassed the men that they were not quite sure what to do next. There was much clearing of throats and coughing. The uniformed officer drummed his fingers on the window pane. They had expected a tiger-like roar, an explosion of tears, a supplication for mercy, a complete confession and instead felt as though they had interrupted a child at its bedtime prayers.

'Yes — er — well, hum — you — er — will have every opportunity later to — er —hum — say prayers for your departed father,' one of the three men in civilian clothes said. 'You — er — may visit the — er — prison chapel afterwards and attend Mass if you so wish. But — hum — meanwhile, we would like you to tell us all about that silly organization of yours.'

'What are the names of the people who worked for the organization?' the man in the centre asked.

'Vielleicht will die Rotznase etwas essen. Versuchen Sie vielleicht das. Und um Gotteswillen, machen Sie's schnell. Ich muss doch weg.' The officer snapped his orders at the civilians, telling them to try offering Lydia food in an attempt to obtain their required information and he told them to hurry the proceedings up as he had to leave soon.

The sound of the German gutteral voice clicked upon the tearducts of Lydia's brain and, at last, she wept. The tears came bitterly, quickly. She cried for her father, sobbing into her hands, her back bent almost double into her lap.

'Now, come, come,' said the man in the middle. 'Crying won't help. Your father won't come back to life just because you produce tears. Give us the names and we shall give you lots of good food and allow you to have parcels sent to you from your friends outside. So you see, my dear, all you have to do is to co-operate a little with us. Now then, what about those names, eh?'

Names, names, names. All they could ask was for names when all the time her father was dead, shot by them. But Lydia did not speak. She just kept on sobbing loudly — and she kept on thinking. This was all a repetition of the previous interview she had, the interview that ended up with that cigarette being pressed against her neck, burning through the skin with the most terrible pain she had ever experienced. She could still feel the burning of it, could still feel the cut skin and the blisters that would mark her for a long time. If they had arrested all those who worked for the *reseau* 'F 1', if they had killed most of them already as she had been told, and if they were all to be killed shortly, what earthly use could it be for her to give them the names? Between her sobs Lydia gave her answer.

'I — I don't know. I don't know any names. Oh, please leave me alone.'

'Take her away, quick,' rapped the man in the middle of the group behind the table and, for the first time since she had entered the room, Lydia realized that the wardress who had brought her was still standing there. The hand of Brunnhilde pounded on her shoulder and dragged her to her feet, swivelled her round and marched her out.

'You silly little fool,' said the wardress once they were outside. 'Don't you realize that you'll have to go through all that again and that it will be a lot worse next time? Why don't you tell them and get the whole blasted thing over with?' Brunnhilde's hand grip relaxed and she led Lydia back to her cell. In the woman's voice there was a mixture of motherly reproach and kindness. She was, after all, French and Lydia was, after all, no more than a child whose father had been killed for being a patriot.

The interrogations continued just as Brunnhilde had prophesied. Each day Lydia was taken to the oak-panelled room and each day two or three men would try to drag a confession out of her. The inquisitions lasted between four and six hours every day and went on ruthlessly for one week. Brunnhilde was also right when she said the interviews would become worse. Questions were now accompanied by hard-hand slaps across Lydia's face. She was punched in the ribs and in the back until she could hardly breathe. But despite this cruelty, she refused to betray those who worked for 'F 1' or any of the other networks. If her father was dead, Lydia thought, then she must continue his fight for him.

Instead of replying, Lydia cried and cried. She found that tears were her best defensive weapon and always continued to believe that her persecutors thought she genuinely knew nothing and that she was only a soft child who had been nurtured on nothing but milk and knew only how to cry. Her tears were genuine enough for the pain that was handed out to her was more than any girl of sixteen could bear. And then there was the pain in her heart for Lydia realized that she was completely alone. Her father had been killed, no doubt ruthlessly — for the Germans were not known for their humane killing of hostages or spies. She had heard how people had been strung up on scaffoldings, hung by their legs upside down and whipped until they were almost dead, then shot and left to rot for the whole world to see. Placards would be hung from their bodies. 'This was a traitor to France' would be the slogan scrawled on the notice. Often, she heard, it had been written in the man's own blood.

But the Germans kept their promise to her. After her first interview at the Santé, she was given food in her cell. At least, they called it food. A watery soup that was no more than the drained water from boiled potatoes, a crust of stale bread that was sometimes so old that a green fungus had grown over it, and a mug of ersatz coffee. On Sundays the meals were better. After Mass in the prison chapel, a plate of tasteless potatoes and a thin slice of undercooked meat and a few leaves of cabbage would be brought to her.

And once a month she was able to receive a parcel from friends outside. The first one came as a surprise to her. She had given up all hope of anyone knowing where she was or even knowing that she was still alive. She thought that all her friends had been arrested by the Germans. But the parcel arrived and was handed to her with the post the other prisoners received. The first parcel had come from Mademoiselle Rita Gautier, an old friend of the Lipski family who was to remain Lydia's dearest friend throughout her ten long lonely months in that cramped cell at the Santé. What luxury that brown paper package contained! There was fruit — two apples and two pears — some boiled potatoes in a little cardboard container, a slice of margarine and a few slices of good bread. Lydia could hardly believe her eyes and her stomach groaned in gratitude. Her eyes devoured the banquet before her and a tiny stream of saliva trickled from the corner of her mouth.

Lydia planned the meal with the care of a cordon bleu chef preparing his menu for the president of the Republic. First she would eat one of the delicious looking potatoes. Just one. The rest she would keep for the evening when she could have it with the thin vegetable soup they would serve her. She would follow the potato with one slice of bread and a thin layer of margarine. This would leave her another slice for the evening meal and she would save the rest of the margarine and bread for the next day.

She planned to end the luxury repast with one of the apples. The other apple and the two pears would be kept for the rest of the week. Perhaps, she thought, just one bite every day, one little bite could make the fruit last a good week or even two weeks. It was the best tasting meal Lydia had ever eaten in her life and even the weak ersatz coffee she was given by the warder, seemed to contain a flavour she had never before noticed. After her feasts, Lydia performed a little dance round her cell. It was the first time she had danced since her arrest. There was nothing choreographically artistic in that dance. It was more of a hop-skip-jump, it's-great-to-be-alive performance, but to Lydia it was a dance that contained all the emotions she had kept locked up within her. She was thin, her hair was bedraggled, her clothes were in shreds — but in her eyes there was a light burning rays of happiness and content.

That evening she was to perform an even happier dance.

The warder brought the plate of soup. As Lydia had rightly forecast, it was the same old vegetable soup, made of water, a few emaciated carrots, rotting potatoes and worm-eaten cabbage leaves. But this time, she was able to eat it as an accompaniment to her potatoes. Her potatoes. 'Come my little potatoes. My stomach awaits you,' sang Lydia and had any normal person seen and heard her without knowing the circumstances, she would most certainly have appeared quite deliriously mad.

Lydia sipped the soup. 'Well, at least it's hot,' she said aloud and sipped some more, eyeing the potatoes that were yet to come, like some child who was being forced to eat up all its spinach before it may start on the favourite pudding. Lydia slowly munched at the round vegetable and closed her eyes. Delicious. Quite delicious. She ate some more of the soup and started on her last potato. And she spat it out.

Lydia's heart missed a beat. She had distinctly felt a piece of paper there in the middle of the potato. Her experience at writing notes in the minutest hand on the thinnest of rice paper and then smuggling those snippets of valuable information out in the strangest ways, made her aware immediately that this could not just be some ordinary piece of paper that had slipped in by accident. She groped in the soft yellow, spat-out potato and fished away the note. There was no mistake about it. It was a note all right, folded up tight into a tiny pellet. Lydia held it tightly in her hand and listened to the sounds around her. There was no unusual noise other than the beating of her own heart. She went to the door and listened. It would not do for a warder to be looking in at her just as she was reading this most important message of all time. What was contained in that piece of wonderful paper? The light was fading fast and only a thin ray of it filtered through the small window of her cell.

Lydia tiptoed towards the light and slowly, gently unfolded the pellet. She felt her heart pounding against her breast and knew that she would have to be prepared to read the worst. It was probably to confirm what the Germans had already told her — that her father was dead and everyone else with the exception of Mademoiselle Gautier who had written the note, arrested, killed, God knows what Lydia was breathing heavily now and felt her hands trembling. The pellet was unfolded. She held it close to her eyes, straining them to make out the miniscule, faint script. And she read. She read and re-read the note and let out a strangled little cry. She fell down upon the straw mattress and wept and wept. Then she rose and danced around her cell as though she was dancing before a king. That night she slept soundly for she wanted the morning to come quickly. She woke up early and the sun was shining, filling her cell with light and warmth. She dragged out from under her dress the note and read it again. No, there was no mistaking it. The dim light of the night before had not deceived her eyes. On the note was written:

'Father safe at Fresnes. Sends his love. God be with you.'

CHAPTER EIGHT:

THE POEM OF LIFE

After that first note, Lydia's attitude to prison life changed. She regained some of her former gaiety, charm and warmth. The weather, too, was changing and the dark clouds that she could see from the floor of her cell gradually disappeared and gave way to the blue of a spring sky. Birds twittered her awake in the mornings and some of them stood at her window looking in at her. Oh, to be like a bird and to be able to fly wherever the wing would take me, thought Lydia and spoke to the birds, telling them her secrets, her thoughts, her desires.

The prison authorities changed too. She was no longer interrogated as regularly as before. They had obviously given her up as a bad job, a girl who knew nothing, who was unable to help them discover the leaders of the network of underground movements that played chaos with the German occupation troops and seemed to know more about the placements of camps and the deployment of troops than even the German Kommandatur. Lydia was given a bed on which to place her straw mattress and a chair on which she could sit. She found that by placing the chair on her bed and moving it all below her window she could climb up, stand on tiptoe and look out into the world below.

There was not much to see. But it was enough. There were the roofs of Paris stretched out before her. She could see chimneys belching out smoke in the distance. Below her was a narrow street and people. People walking about. People strolling in the sun. Lovers, arm in arm on Sundays, walked slowly past staring into each other's eyes as lovers do, and kissing. Girls giggled and men laughed and stroked the hair of their beloved. Lydia saw all this and knew that the world was still awake, that men and women were still alive, still breathing, still strolling up and down the Champs-Elysées just as they had always done.

One day, during her lunch, Lydia climbed up onto her chair on the bed armed with her spoon. She worked hard and long, trying to prise open the little window. It was no easy task. That window had not been opened for years and the wind and rain had made the frame expand and contract so much that it was no longer the shape it was originally given by the builders. Lydia had to give up the job when she heard the warders going from cell to cell collecting empty dishes. But she had not given up the plan to open the window. It took her nearly two week's hard work but eventually she was successful. The window flew open with a little click and a creak and the fresh air of Paris in the spring blew in caressing her nostrils.

She could now hear Paris as well as see it. She was never able to make out conversations in detail as people passed by in the street below, but the hum of conversation was sufficient to make her feel close to those who were making it. She heard the tooting of car horns in the distance and bicycle bells tinkled as merrily as though France was still free. Almost every night the sirens would wail an alert that R.A.F. bombers were flying over the capital and every night Lydia would open her window as wide as possible and try to see the planes as they flew in the darkness of the sky. She sometimes heard their humming and then she prayed that they should drop a few bombs on the prison — just enough to break down the walls and allow all the prisoners to escape.

Being in solitary confinement, Lydia never saw any of the prisoners except on Sundays when they were all herded along to Mass. A tall, thin priest said Mass for them. He said it all in so mechanical a way that he might just as well have been chopping wood as breaking the Host. His face betrayed not a single emotion and the words of his sermon — an Oration that never lasted more than five minutes — were spoken with the enthusiasm of a robot. But however boring the Mass was, the prisoners looked forward to it like children being taken on a school outing. It was a chance to congregate, to feel the closeness of another human being's body to hear human voices making responses in unison.

It was during one of these Sunday treats that Lydia found herself next to a young girl with blonde hair. She could only see the colour of the hair from the corner of her eyes since she was not allowed to look round at the rest of the prisoners. Eagle-eyed warders stood along the aisles of the chapel ready to pounce on any woman who talked or behaved in any way suspiciously. But the young girl who remained an anonymous angel in Lydia's life used the congregational responses to whisper instead of *'Et cum spiritu tuo'* a rapid: 'Are you Lipski?' Lydia waited till the next Amen to answer 'Yes'. During the next two responses, Lydia's ears strained to catch the girl's next remarks. Any conversation had to be rapid for the congregation did not believe in the correct elocution of responses but babbled them off into the wind as automatically as the priest offered his prayers.

'Sursum corda,' ordered the priest.

'Habemus ad Dominum,' mouthed the congregation hardly lifting up their voices let alone their hearts.

'Your window at three,' whispered the blonde at Lydia's side.

'Gratias agamus Domino Deo nostro,' mumbled the priest and blew his nose while the prisoners before him, not knowing for what they were to give thanks, nevertheless murmured in answer: *'Dignum et justum est.'* 'A friend in the street,' said the girl to Lydia.

The only response the congregation shouted out in full unison and with exaggerated fervour was during the Pater Noster when the priest came to *Et ne nos inducas in tentationem* (And lead us not into temptation) all shouted out: *'Sed libera nos a malo'* (But deliver us from evil). This was probably the one part of the whole prayer that every prisoner spoke from the heart, enveloped in every ounce of sincerity. Lydia used the noise to say in a normal voice: 'Bless you and thanks,'

At ten minutes to three that afternoon Lydia, flushed with hope and excitement, placed her chair on the bed and climbed up. She could only guess the time. A church clock in the distance had struck the quarter, half and three-quarters but Lydia did not trust the accuracy of church clocks. One could not trust the accuracy of anything nowadays. For ten long, eternally long minutes, she clung to the bars outside the open window, straining her neck to look down into the street below. Nothing out of the ordinary could be seen. Just the same Sunday strollers, ambling along the street without hurry, without care, their clothes well brushed, shoes shining as best they could after being polished with pieces of newspaper and a rag but no paste. Lydia cursed the vans that passed when at any other time she would have welcomed them. Now they merely obstructed her view. Perhaps she would miss whoever it was that was coming to see her. Who could it be? Surely not her father? No, that was, alas, impossible.

'Oh, if only it could be Papa,' thought Lydia aloud. But he was in Fresnes, another prison. That morning, as indeed every morning, she had prayed that he be safe and well and that the war would soon end and that they would be together again. Her thoughts were interrupted by a familiar face below. She wanted to shout out, cry the name — but stopped herself in time. Any loud commotion would have brought the wardress to the door and one glance through that stupid spy-hole would have wrecked Lydia's secret and probably arrested Rita Gautier below.

For it was Rita, dearest Rita, walking slowly along the street as though she had not a care in the world, Rita who lived to risk her very life by putting notes inside potatoes. Dear Rita Gautier. She was looking up at the prison now, casually, quite casually as though she was glancing over some uninteresting painting by a second-rate artist while walking down one of the corridors of the Louvre. The prison was there, but if Rita Gautier was looking at it for any particular reason, her look did not betray it. Lydia quickly made up her mind and decided to take a risk. She jumped from her chair onto the bed and tore some of the straw from her mattress, climbed back on the chair and flung a handful of the yellow grass out of the window, hoping that there would be no one about other than Rita to see it. Rita Gautier did see it. Her eyes widened for a brief moment of time and her fine mouth formed the suspicion of a smile.

Lydia stuck her right hand through the bars and waved. The movement of her hand caught in the breeze and reflected the warmth of the sun. Rita placed her hand to her mouth, looked round her quickly, and blew a kiss towards the wave. She walked on, turned once more at the corner, smiled in Lydia's direction and disappeared.

From that day on Lydia's mind was at rest. She looked forward to the parcel she would be receiving at the end of the month, looked forward to searching it for another note. Perhaps the next would give her more information than the last — though it certainly could not give her news that was better, unless it were to tell her that her father had been released from prison and that the war was over. Lydia realized after her many hours at her cell window that several of the men and women who were walking in the street below were always the same. She began to recognize faces, walks, even the tone of voices. Could those people below, those people who made it a point to walk in that street at certain times on certain days of the week, could it be that they were friends, that they were members of the Resistance?

She was soon to find out. In the next parcel she received, she found the stub of a pencil embedded in the hollow of an apple, sheets of paper neatly folded between the wrappings of the packages — and a note, once again in one of the potatoes.

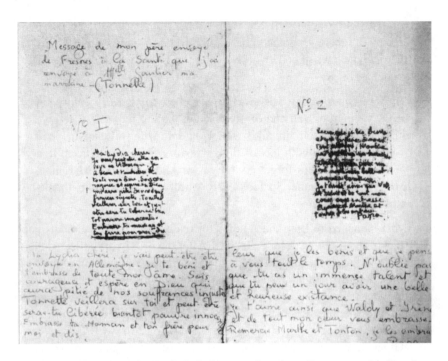

12. One of the messages Lydia's father sent her from Fresnes to the Sauté through Gautier, (Tonnette), It reads: 'My darling Lydia, I shall perhaps be sent to Germany. I bless you and kiss you with all my soul. Be courageous and hope in God who will have pity on our unjust suffering. Tonnette will look after you and perhaps you will soon be freed my poor innocent. Kiss your mother and your brother for me and tell them that I send them my blessings and that I think of you all, all the time. Do not forget that you have great talents and that one day you can have a beautiful and happy existence. I love you and Waldy (her brother) and Irène (her mother) and embrace the three of you with all my heart. Thank Marthe (Madame Bertheaux) and Tonton (Tonnette). I kiss them. Signed Papa.'

'Father sends love. All's well. Throw messages from window 1500 hours daily. Keep smiling. God bless.' The note burned life into Lydia and she treasured the pencil and the paper she had been sent even more than the food. She wrote message after message. Each day, rolled into a neat little ball, she would throw the paper down into the street. It was always picked up, always delivered. Lydia's letters were written in the greatest detail and in the smallest, finest hand. She would sharpen the pencil with her finger nails and along the stone wall. She wrote of her life in prison — or, rather, of her lack of life there — notes to her father, to her friends — always giving only Christian names or code words — and she would write silly little notes. Notes such as these:

> 'My loved ones: today was just like any other day here — empty but for the thought of you and of my darling, darling father. Please give him my love and tell him all is well. Could do with some lipstick and powder. Could do with lots of things: soap, a mirror, a tablecloth, a pair of gloves. Don't forget give my love André, Juliette, Marianne, Jean, Paul, Christiane. So looking forward parcels. Trillions thanks and love: Cipinka.'

Lydia managed to keep those notes for many years. The recipients kept each one of them safely, despite the risks. After the war, Lydia collected them together and they were later to be found in her father's private museum.

When the next parcel arrived, Lydia pounced on it hardly daring to wait to find what message would be inside. She had unwrapped it and was just examining an apple, when the door opened and the wardress she called Brunnhilde entered.

'All right, you, let's have a look what is inside that parcel of yours...' Brunnhilde carried a knife in her hand. Lydia had emptied the contents of the parcel out onto the chair and was kneeling down beside it. Brunnhilde bent down over the food. Lydia could smell the woman. Like so many fat women, Brunnhilde smelled of stale sweat and the echo of a garlic garnished meal still hung on her breath. She cut through the apple Lydia had been holding when she came in. There was nothing except apple. She then sliced one of the two pears in half.

'You may have half my pear — if — if you like,' said Lydia smiling generously at Brunnhilde and hoping that pears were as good a bribe as any these austere days.

'Thanks,' said Brunnhilde and stuffed the half pear into her mouth and bit through it. Holding the remainder in her left hand she set about the potatoes. There were seven potatoes in all in the little white cardboard container. They had been carefully boiled and a little brown gravy had been poured over them and floated in the bottom of the box. Brunnhilde cut through the first potato and Lydia's heart pounded away fiercely.

Brunnhilde swallowed her pear and threw the rest of her half in to her mouth. The juice ran out of the corner of her mouth and she wiped it away with the sleeve of her arm. 'Good pears, these,' she commented professionally and continued cutting the potatoes. But after cutting up five, she gave up, got to her feet with a groan of age and stiffness, shrugged her ample shoulders and, still chewing at the pear, left the cell, crashing the door shut behind her. Lydia breathed a sigh of deep relief. Nothing had been found. But perhaps there was nothing.

Lydia examined the remaining two potatoes. In one of them she found a note. She unravelled it carefully. The handwriting was familiar — but it was not from Rita Gautier.

It was from her father.

It was from her father and it was a poem, written in neat pencil lines, a poem he had composed at Fresnes Prison. Through hot, blinding tears, Lydia read it. It was entitled

'To Lydia.'
Do not cry, my child, should you see all hopes of happiness
Disappear so suddenly from all your dreams,
For one day soon God Himself will dispel your distress
And give your heart once more the means
To laugh.
If love has wounded you and you suffer, alas —
Do not cry.
But if one winter's eve when all is sad
And your soul has suffered and your heart feels low,
Come then, o come to the refuge of my arms.
With love they will be open.
And, pressed against me as of days gone by,
You may cry. Yes, then you may cry.'*

Lydia had never thought of her father as a romantic poet before. He was just her father, the man who had helped bring her into the world, had fed and clothed her, brought her up to be God-fearing, taught her that beauty was truth, truth beauty and, when the war came and she had decided to stay with him and fight for the freedom of France, it was her father who had nursed her into fearlessness, had created out of a child the woman — straight-backed, proud and cunning, a spy who had never attended a school for spies. Now here, for the first time, was a poem that elevated Wladimir de Korczak Lipski from the ideal father figure into the romantic knight in shining armour, the

---

*A selection of other poems written by Wladimir de Korezak Lipski at Fresnes and, later, at Mauthausen concentration camp appears in Appendix One.

existentialist, the man of reason and of heart who would fight despite all the odds against him — the man who had not forgotten the child who had turned woman and who now languished in a cold prison that was called Health.

With that poem, Lydia's loneliness slipped from her with the same abandon as when the albatross fell from round the Ancient Mariner's neck. She felt that her prayers had been answered and knelt down to weep her thanks to Heaven and ask forgiveness for having ever doubted the powers of God and of Right and of Justice.

It had taken Lydia longer than normal to befriend other prisoners at La Santé. She was unable to see them for she was not allowed to mingle with them. Her routine was different from the others. Apart from Sunday Mass, she saw no one except the wardresses. These would come for her at odd moments during the day to escort her to her inquisitors, to take her for her weekly shower and her daily ablutions. Loneliness and anguish played on Lydia's nerves more than anything else. But, once she had made contact with the outside world, once she had realized that her father was not dead and that her nightmares had lied to her, she took a greater interest in the walls around her. She realized, for instance, that there was another girl in the next cell. Perhaps it was the same girl who had given her that helpful information at Mass. The walls were too thick to be able to speak through them, but Lydia and the unknown face next door struck up a friendship nevertheless. They tapped messages to each other through the concrete. Lydia invented the code. It was the simplest code in the world.

One tap on the wall represented 'A', two taps spelled 'B', three 'C' and so on through the alphabet. It took the best part of a day to put across the meaning of this code, but eventually the girl in the next cell responded that she had understood. The tapping friendship blossomed.

'I am called Lydia,' tapped Lydia slowly, closing her eyes tightly to concentrate on the counting and the spelling. 'Your name, please.'

Slowly the reply came back: 'Lonique.' A second attempt changed this to Monique. Monique was four years older than Lydia and, the taps told, had celebrated her twentieth birthday inside the prison. She was there because she had been arrested for black marketeering and for slapping a German soldier's face. He had exposed himself before her and then kissed her. She slapped out in fury. They had arrested her for this crime and had found out about the black market deals on further investigations. French women, however promiscuous, do not abide vulgarity. It was not so much the fact of a German soldier trying to have intercourse with Monique that put her in a rage. It was the way in which he did it. French girls have to be wooed for a fairly long time before they will give themselves to a man. No slap-and-tickle nonsense about the French. 'So I slap him,' read Monique's simple taps.

After some days of facts — names, addresses, reasons for being in prison (Lydia told Monique the reasons for her own arrest in the barest outline only) — the messages became more intimate, the confidences of two school girls who are just awakening to the wide world of sex.

'I dream last night again of same man,' Monique spelled out on the wall. 'He was here in cell with me. Made love to me. Kissed me all over. He said he loved me. But I wake up all wet and uncomfortable. Wish I was out then would get real man. Perhaps he comes again tonight.'

Lydia envied Monique her dreams. Admittedly, her nightmares had not been as frequent now that she knew her father to be safe, but her dreams were not exciting like the other girl's. She dreamed of taking walks in the country with her father, of bathing in the sea at Nice where the sun was so warm but the sea was so cold, so very cold and she could not manage to gather up the warmth of the sun. She would wake up sweating and shivering in the cold dampness of her cell. She did not have sexual dreams for the simple reason that she had never experienced sex. There were admittedly those times when the boys with whom she danced at the ballet school would grab her by her small young breasts instead of round her waist as they were supposed to do. Some tried to date her. Some even tried to kiss her.

The pecked kisses she had accepted in good grace. They had meant nothing to her. But she remembered the time when one of the boys at the school had caught hold of her in the dark passage way leading from the school into the street. 'Come on Lydia,' he had said. 'Give me a kiss.' She had laughed her usual tinkle of a laugh and answered. 'All right, just one.' It was the same peck she allowed herself with all the others who had asked her similar favours. But suddenly the boy clasped her tighter. 'No, no, Lydia. A real kiss. Look, like this.' And he pressed his lips hard against her own, forcing open her mouth with his sharp tongue. Lydia struggled. Somehow she felt revolted against this boy's strange behaviour. She had never been kissed like that before. It seemed terribly unhygienic, such a kiss. His tongue had forced an entry to her mouth. It was terrible. Lydia pounded her fists against the boy's shoulders and, with an extra effort, twisted herself free. *'Vous—vous êtes un salaud'*, was all she could think to say to the boy before fleeing in tears pursued only by the loud laughter of her would-be lover. Now in her prison the memory of that kiss returned. Perhaps, thought Lydia, perhaps it was not all that bad after all. And she, too, wished she could have such dreams as Monique's.

But the dreams did not come. Instead of handsome rescuers pushing aside the bars of her cell and snatching her to freedom with a kiss, she dreamed of white Christmases and of the sea. Mostly she dreamed of the sea. And the sea was no longer the beautiful blue of the Mediterranean but a swirling black sucking her under. The only caress Lydia felt, was the cold, clammy caress of a stormy ocean. She felt herself drowning. The water engulfed her. She tried to swim but her arms would not move. Her legs felt weak, unable to strike out against the weight of the waves. When she awoke she was gasping for breath. Her breathing became more and more difficult as the weeks went on. Her legs were as weak as they felt in her dreams. She could barely find the strength to tap messages to Monique any more. Lydia was sick. Even Brunnhilde noticed how ill she was when she brought in the breakfast one morning. Lydia had been in the cell for ten months. She was no longer able to differentiate between the days. Sometimes it came as quite a surprise to her when they opened the door to take her to Mass. She realized then that it was Sunday. The dampness of her cell did not help matters. In order to keep warm even on summer nights, she walked round and round the eleven by six feet stone box like some wild animal at the zoo. Her cell was just like a cage. She often thought of herself as a poor caged lioness, sturdy of heart but completely helpless and unhappy in her imprisonment.

There was no mirror in the cage and Lydia did not really know what she looked like. Sometimes, when dusk was falling over the city, throwing eerie shadows over the sun and making midgets seem like giants, she would stand on the chair on her bed and heave herself up to the window encrusted in dust. At that strange point between light and total darkness, that point when everything is silent and even the trees do not breathe, Lydia was able to see herself in the glass. She saw a ghost. It was not the same Lydia who skipped home from her dancing lessons, nor even the Lydia who worked late into the night copying plans of German installations to send to England. This Lydia was different. This Lydia of the dirty glass was haggard and deathly pale and when she grinned at herself to see whether she could still grin, she could see no teeth reflected though she knew that she still had her teeth. She found it difficult to make out her eyes, too. Yet she was able to see. She was seeing the ghost of herself — she was seeing her own future as an old hag, dead, white, cold, toothless, eyeless, a skull, decayed and a lonely tear would creep down her sagging cheek and mingle with the tears wept by the walls.

But now, now after she had given up all hope of seeing the outside world again, given up the will to fight against the damp and the cold and the bars and the walls, now Lydia was ill. She was unable to breathe properly. It hurt her chest. Pains like the stings of young nettles pricked her. Brunnhilde, big and fat and smelly, found Lydia stretched out on the thing they called a bed, her thin arm flopped over the side and hanging down like a dead branch.

'Hey, Lipski, you all right? What's the matter with you? Lipski?' Brunnhilde received no reply and thought for a moment that Lydia was dead. Brunnhilde was a funny sort. She did not mind torturing a prisoner, kicking and punching her until she lost consciousness. Brunnhilde rather liked drawing blood. It gave her a thrill. She admitted it to her fellow wardresses. 'When I punch their noses in, why shit, I enjoy seeing the blood run. I feel I want to bathe in it,' she confessed. 'I don't really mean those poor bastards any harm. It's just that I like — I don't know — I just like seeing 'em bleed and cry.' But death—Brunnhilde was afraid of death. She enjoyed half-killing her prisoners but hated to see them die. No prisoner had ever died on Brunnhilde, and very few gave her cause to beat them up. Now, standing before Lydia and seeing her lying there so still and flopped, Brunnhilde saw no other reason than that she was dead. A chill hand passed over her spine and she felt sweat under her hairy arm-pits. Her lips went quite dry and she wished she had not come into that cell but had stayed with her bottle of pastis which one of the Germans had given her. She went closer to Lydia, frightened to touch her in case she was already stiff and cold and hard like her father was when he died when fat Brunnhilde was still only a child and her mother had made her touch him.

Lydia stirred slightly and Brunnhilde could hear her breathing now. Her face flushed with anger and embarrassment. 'Lipski, get up you silly bastard,' she said and thought what a cheek to put the wind up her like that. Now she felt like lashing out and kicking the living daylights out of this snip of a girl who had scared her. 'Get up, d'you hear.'

But Lydia only moaned a little and Brunnhilde knew that she was not having her on. She was really ill. 'All right then, stay where you are. Damn little bitch. You've been nothing but trouble since the day you came here.' But Brunnhilde, still sweating and her heart thumping with a mixture of leftover fear and relief, slammed the door shut and went for the prison doctor.

Lydia was examined and taken to the infirmary which was already overcrowded with the sick and pregnant. They brought her fever down by shoving a few suppositories up her and then gave her an X-ray. This showed that she had contracted a mild form of tuberculosis. There was a definite spot on one of her lungs. Three weeks later, when the pneumonia had subsided and Lydia was able to eat and drink again, the doctor decided that she must be moved out of the Santé. T.B. was too much trouble for him. There was nothing unusual about it, but it was easier to pass the buck to someone else.

'You are going to be sent to Fresnes,' the doctor told Lydia one morning. 'You'd better get ready.'

Fresnes! Lydia could not believe her good fortune. Had the doctor hold her she was going to be sent to the Riviera or to Paradise, he could not have given her better news. Fresnes was where her father was. 'Oh, thank you, Monsieur, thank you, thank you so very much,' she said and the doctor shrugged his shoulders failing to understand her gratitude. The girl must be mad as well as sick he thought and returned to his quarters and a good lunch of chicken cooked in white wine.

CHAPTER NINE:

CELL MATES AT FRESNES

Fresnes turned out to be a little better than La Santé. Lydia was taken to a cell that looked almost like a hotel room compared with the cage she had at her first prison. There were three beds in the cell and the walls were whitewashed and clean looking. The window was not as high up as her old one and she was able to look out by just standing on a chair. Admittedly, the view was not as interesting for it overlooked the court-yard of the prison and not the street but one was able to see across to the other blocks and make conversation with women prisoners there.

What was even better, Lydia shared her cell with two other women, Colette and Jeanne. The latter was a resistance worker like Lydia and the two were able to exchange experiences of the days when both were working against the Nazi conquerors. Colette was a prostitute, shapely but slovenly, whose beauty had known better days and who did not believe in mincing her words about what she thought of the Germans.

But if Lydia thought that she was going to see her father, she was mistaken. After three weeks at Fresnes she found out that he had left the jail a matter of a few days before she had come to it. No one seemed to know where he had been sent, but everyone seemed to think that he might be at a work camp inside France.

'I wish they'd send me to a work camp,' offered Jeanne trying to cheer her latest friend up. 'They say that there one can eat as much as one wants. Most of the camps are attached to farms and the prisoners help the farmers with their harvests or planting and sowing. The farmers are French, after all

Lydia, so they treat the workers all right. I heard of one man who went to one of these camps and he grew so fat after a few months, he actually had to go on a diet.'

'Who wants to diet?' asked Colette. 'If they sent me to one of those places I'd eat myself sick and keep my figure by exercise.'

'Yes, sure,' said Jeanne. 'We all know what exercise you mean' And all three laughed.

Colette was well into her thirties and Jeanne was thirty-two. This made Lydia the baby of the cell and both the other women competed with each other in their attempts to mother her. 'Now come along *mon p'tit chou*, time to have a nap. Lie down and go to sleep. We want you to leave here rich in health if not in wealth,' one or the other would say and tuck Lydia into her hard but infinitely more comfortable bed than she had slept in at the Santé. The two women would sit in silence while Lydia slept, watching over her like hens over their brood, cooing over her with pride. Both women had always wanted to bear children but never did, so Lydia's arrival was to them the answer of their prayers. She was someone for them to love and to hold.

Lydia had spent her seventeenth birthday in the solitude of her cell at the Santé, cold and hungry and alone. She had not even realized that it was her birthday until it was almost over. Then she had cried. There had never been a birthday quite like it. No friends to come and drink her health and give her presents, no cake, no candles, no laughter and songs. Nothing. A void, all darkness and silence, empty, pitilessly empty.

Her eighteenth birthday was different. Colette and Jeanne had been preparing themselves for this day almost from the moment they had found out Lydia's age and the date of her birth. As January 8, 1943, drew near, the women pooled their food. Each put a potato or a piece of bread and margarine aside, keeping the hoard stocked in a tin box one of them managed to scrounge from one of the other prisoners. Cigarette ends were carefully kept. So was the fruit and cake they had received from their relations outside in their monthly parcel. Lydia had eaten her parcel contents already and had again found the precious note which she read out to her friends. It told her that her father was safe, not to worry and that all friends sent their love to her and that the war would not last much longer. *'Vive la France,'* said Colette without emotion after Lydia had finished reading, had screwed the piece of paper into a ball and swallowed it, just as she had done with all the other messages she had received.

'Oh, what I wouldn't give to see the end of the war,' said Colette with a dreamy look in her eyes. *'Merde*, there'd be fun and games then. I'd kick each boche hard where it hurts most and see to it that they'd never be able to make love again, not to anyone, the bastards...'

On January 8 Lydia awoke to the cooing of 'Happy birthday, *chérie*' and was kissed affectionately by Colette and Jeanne in turn. That evening they brought out their presents.

'It's not very much, I'm afraid, Lydia,' said Jeanne with great embarrassment, 'but, well, the shops were closed when I got to them and this was all.' Colette and Jeanne then placed their offerings on the little table in their cell. There were apples and potatoes looking a little tired, cake and biscuits that had turned hard and soft in turn, a greying piece of chocolate and twelve cigarette ends. Lydia was speechless. She looked at the presents and then up at the two women looking at her with love and pride and expectancy and burst into tears.

'What's the matter Lydia? Don't you like them?' said Colette and she and Jeanne exchanged glances filled with woe. Lydia managed to explain between sobs. 'Of — course — I like them — they're wonderful. It's — it's just — that I'm so — ha — happy.'

'Well, you've got a funny way of showing it,' said Colette, wiping away the moisture from her own eyes.

Come along then Lydia, let's tuck in,' Jeanne said quietly and took Lydia gently by the shoulders. It reminded Jeanne of her own childhood. She had come from a poor family. Her father worked on the Metro, punching tickets. Her mother went to the fine houses out at Neuilly as a *femme de ménage,* scrubbing and cleaning for next to nothing. She did not know where her father was now but had an idea that he was working for the Maquis somewhere in Central France. Her brother had gone off to England in answer to General de Gaulle's call and had joined the Free French Army. Jeanne did not know whether he was dead or alive. As for her mother, she did not know where she was at all. Perhaps they had taken her to a concentration camp. She had no idea. But to see Lydia crying reminded her of her own birthdays when her parents had scraped together a few francs to buy her a new frock or a pullover. There was always something for her despite the family's poverty and she recalled that she, too, had cried with joy to see that her parents still cared enough for her to buy her something they could not afford. Her father spoke of the day when France would become Communist just like Russia. 'That's when we'll have plenty,' he used to say. 'The capitalists won't be able to treat us like slaves for ever. There'll come the day when the workers will be able to live properly and won't need to worry where the next meal is going to come from, you wait and see.'

Instead of a Red Revolution, however, the Nazis came to France and she recalled how her father had sat down and cried. And she remembered how he had cursed the Germans and the world for his disappointment had been great. And he had cursed the French, too, when he saw the mass exodus from Paris, the panic as people threw all their worldly goods onto carts, wheelbarrows and into sacks and began the endless trek out to the country. The trains were so packed, people were hanging on by their finger nails and even sitting on the roofs. Old women and children tramped a route towards the unknown. 'They'll pay for this, the weak, stupid cowards,' her father had said. 'They'll pay for this. Never ever let me catch you running away from anything, Jeanne. These people are fools. They don't know where they're going or when they're going to arrive there. They're travelling in a false hope, traitors to their hearts, their families and their country. When we have driven the *boche* out of France and that shouldn't take too long — these wretches will be back begging for their homes, crying out for their shops and their goods. They'll be thieving and lying and blaming it all on the *boche* when it's really all their own fault. The fools, the silly, stupid fools. They don't understand. They just don't understand. And, to tell you the truth, my little Jeanne, I'm not so sure if I understand it all either...'

Now here she was, little Jeanne, in prison for trying to do as her father had said and not run away from her conscience. She had done her little bit to help France regain her honour. Here she was, locked up in a cell with a child and a prostitute. Jeanne, unmarried, unloved. Forgotten by the outside world. Just another number in the prison register and giving a little pleasure to a girl who reminded her of her childhood.

And Colette—black-haired Colette the coquette, looked down at Lydia and thought of the child she so desperately wanted. She had been an only child herself. Her father, though not rich, was well off. He was a traveller for a big firm that manufactured household goods — everything for the house, from kitchen pots and pans to bathroom soap holders. She only saw him once or twice a week when he came home. Other children at the school made fun of her because they said her father was only the lodger and did she have more than one mummy. Kids! Her mother was not in the house all that often either. They lived near the Gare du Nord. Her mother used to go out a lot. 'There's a bit of fish in the ice box, Colette. Now mind you go to bed early, d'you hear. I'm meeting some friends this evening and expect I'll be a bit late. Good night, darling.' There was a hurried peck and Colette could smell her mother's perfume. She liked the smell of that perfume.

One night she woke up and heard giggling from her mother's room. She heard a man's voice and, thinking her father had come home, ran towards the giggles. 'Daddy, Daddy...' she called. But it was not her father. It was some other man whom she had never seen before. Her mother had slapped her face and sent her back to bed. She remembered seeing that her mother was naked and she thought the man had nothing on either. Later on her mother had come to her room wearing her night dress under a dressing-gown, the pure silk red one her father had given her the last Christmas. 'You shouldn't come into Mummy's bedroom like that, sweetheart. One of your uncles is staying here tonight. He was just passing through Paris. He may have to leave early but he has given me something to buy you a nice present. So you go to sleep now. Mummy is very sorry she slapped you just now, but Mummy was very angry with her little girl for being naughty. Now you forget all about it, eh? There's a good darling.' But Colette did not forget. She liked the present though and received several other presents on other occasions. She heard the uncle several times again but she thought, sometimes, that his voice was different. All she knew was that she should not tell Daddy. She did not know why. No one had asked her not to. But an instinct told her that if she told Daddy, she would not get any more presents. Besides, another instinct told her that Daddy would be very hurt if she told him an uncle had slept in his bed with Mummy, and she would not have liked to hurt Daddy.

She became quite used to hearing men in her mother's room and noticed that, besides having presents for herself, there were various other new things about the house — new tablecloths, cushions, curtains and more mirrors in Mummy's room. Mummy, herself, wore better clothes and looked lovelier than ever before. She wore different kinds of perfume, too, not just the same one. And the larder was much fuller than usual. There were always eggs and a chicken or two and biscuits and various salamis and once she even found a half-empty jar of something called caviar. And there were bottles of champagne and loads of wine and boxes of cigarettes that played music when you opened the lid.

Colette grew up accepting her mother's visitors because of the presents she received herself twice or even three times a week. There were dolls and chocolates and little bracelets and sweets. And when Daddy came home, he would bring her presents as well. So everything was all right. None of the uncles ever came when Daddy was there and Mummy never went out either, but the giggling went on just the same. But Colette still didn't go to her mother's bedroom, even though she knew for certain that it was her father who was in there.

And then, just after Colette had reached the age of fourteen, her mother had come into her bedroom. Colette could see that her mother had been crying but did not know why. But she said nothing because she could hear a man humming some popular tune of the day in the next room.

'Colette, my love, there's a gentleman who would like very much to meet you. He is very nice, really. I'm sure you will like him. Slip something on and come and say hello.' Colette remembered that her mother did not look at her as she always did when she spoke to her, but had her back turned when she told her about the gentleman. And she had not even called him an uncle. Colette had known for a long time now that the men who paid her mother all these visits were not really her uncles but she still did not protest when her mother referred to them as such. She also knew that these men were making love to her mother. She had never been taught any of the facts of life properly but she had picked up enough from her school friends to know what was what. She got out of bed without a murmur, slipped on a dressing-gown her mother had thrown on the bed and put on her slippers.

In the living-room sat a man. She could not even remember what he looked like except that he was greying at the temples and was drinking cognac out of a balloon glass. He looked at her all over and told her to come and sit down with her mother and him. Then he poured her a glass of cognac. She remembered how her mother had protested: 'No, no Charles, not so much. She's only a child. You'll get her drunk.' But Charles just laughed and said. 'Nonsense, it'll do her good, won't it, *ma p'tit?*' She drank a little of the alcohol and it made her cough a lot and choke.

She remembered how, later, she felt giddy and her mother took her back to bed and kissed her. The next day Colette felt very giddy and had a headache. But her mother had given her a present which she said had been left by the gentleman called Charles. How nice of him! How nice.

A few evenings later, there was a ring at the door. Colette was alone and was just going to bed. She went to the door and found Charles there. '*Maman* is out, Monsieur,' she said and felt a little scared. But Monsieur Charles just smiled. 'That's all right. I'll wait for her.' And he came in and sat down. 'Well, aren't you going to offer me a drink, little Colette?' She brought him the bottle of Remy Martin and a glass, but the man made her get herself a glass too. 'Have one to keep me company. It'll make you sleep better,' he had said and filled her glass. She didn't like the drink because it had made her choke again. Then Charles said it was time for little girls to be in bed and that he would come and tuck her in. He did, too. When she was in bed he came in. And he was all naked and Colette cried a little and then the man hurt her a bit and kissed her all over and called her his beloved and his beauty and said how much he had always wanted her and asked whether she didn't care a little for him. And Colette just cried and was afraid and wished her mother would come. But her mother didn't come. When Charles left, he gave Colette 200 francs and said he would give her more next time.

The next morning there was a bit of blood in her bed but Colette didn't have any headache like the last time she had drunk brandy and she did have 200 francs — and 200 francs was a lot of money. She did not tell her mother about Monsieur Charles' visit or what had happened. She threw the sheet into the dirty linen box and put a fresh one on her bed. She noticed that her mother looked at her strangely, even anxiously, but she said nothing to her. And the next time Monsieur Charles came he brought a friend with him. Her mother was out again.

Monsieur Charles gave her 300 francs this time and the other man gave her 350 francs....

But she was never able to have any children. She could never bring a baby into the world and bring it up to be good and respect humanity. She so wanted a child of her own so that she could teach it goodness and bring it up to be what she was not. And Colette had lost all respect for humanity. She had even lost her respect for her own mother.

Now they were together. Jeanne, good little Jeanne who thought she was contributing something towards the freedom of France so that her father could realize his ideals and bring Communism and happiness to the workers; and *la pauvre petite* Lydia all innocence and beauty, thrown into a world of war and greed, smashed against the walls of a prison because she had played a spying game.

And the three of them laughed and ate their apples and cake and potatoes and smoked their dimps. It was a good party. A very good party.

'So what are you going to do when the war's over, eh, Lydia?'

Lydia thought for a moment, puffing away at her cigarette and coughing because she had not smoked before and because she still found it a little difficult to breathe easily. 'Well, first of all, I shall cook the most wonderfully big meal for my father and mother and brother and we'll have the most fabulous reunion France has ever seen. And I shall invite both of you to come along to it, because — well, you're part of my family now, aren't you? And then, afterwards, I shall take myself off for a holiday to Nice or St. Raphael and swim in the sea and get my body all sunburned. Then, when I've had a good rest, I shall return to Paris and go on with my dancing. I should like to dance like my mother. She's a fabulously good dancer. You should have seen her in The Dying Swan. Well, actually, I've never seen her dance it myself, but I've photographs of her dancing it and they say she was just as good as Pavlova any day. Maybe, one day, I shall dance The Dying Swan at the Opera. Yes, I think I'll dance at the Opera...'

'What if there's no opera house left for you to dance in *chérie*?' asked Jeanne.

'The Opera will always be there,' replied Lydia with confidence. 'But if they won't have me,' she smiled, 'then I shall form my own group and we shall have a theatre all of our own. If we could do it during the war, we should certainly be able to do it in peace time. But if that should fail, well then I'd dance anywhere for anyone as long as it's here in France.'

'Even at the Folies-Bergère?' asked Colette.

'And what's the matter with the Folies-Bergère?' replied Lydia. 'It would be an honour to dance there. Just think of all the others who made their name there. There was the great Josephine Baker herself. She made her name at the Folies...'

'Oh, listen to the child,' said Colette. 'She wants to dance at the Folies.' And she lifted up her skirts and accompanied herself in a mock can-can round the cell.

No, Colette, no, not like that. Look, this is how you do it.' And Lydia, her skirt held high above her waist, danced a can-can while Jeanne and Colette clapped their hands and sang Offenbach's can-can music from *La Vie Parisienne*. No cell at Fresnes had rung out with so much music and happiness in its history. But the dance was cut short by the warders who rapped on the door.

'What the hell's going on in there. Shut up the lot of you or you'll all be in solitary till you rot,' a warder commanded.

'We're celebrating,' Colette shouted back. 'Can't one even celebrate nowadays?'

'Celebrating? Celebrating what?'

'The end of the war and the death to all boche bastards,' laughed Colette. Jeanne and Lydia joined in the laughter and listened to the warders moving away cursing under their breath.

The girls really believed that the war could not last much longer. News had trickled in from the outside that the Germans were having heavy losses on all fronts. The Russians and the Americans had joined up with Britain and Hitler was having to fight his battles against heavy odds. It would not be long, the girls thought before Hitler was destroyed and the Allies would liberate France and the rest of oppressed Europe.

Lydia firmly believed this to be true, too. The Germans were hardly ever interviewing her now. Sometimes she was called for. About once every three or four weeks and the same questions would be shot at her. Her face would be slapped a few times and then she would be allowed to go back to her cell and her friends. It almost seemed as though the Germans were asking her all those questions merely to give themselves an excuse for having arrested her and keeping her arrested. It stopped them losing face that way. Lydia hated the Germans but she played along with them in their little game, giving them the same old answers in exchange for a few slaps.

Lydia's cough was getting better too. Her breathing was easier and Jeanne and Colette heaved sighs of relief whenever a day went by that Lydia did not cough or complain about her breathing . 'It's not much of a convalescent home, this, but it seems to have done you quite well, *ma p'tite*' said Colette.

But the good days were not to last. Lydia was called before the prison commandant one morning after she had been at Fresnes for nearly a year and told that she was to be sent away to the country for a spell. Lydia thought that the man was joking. The country? Maybe they had given up trying to make her talk. Maybe they thought they had made a big mistake about her and were trying to make it up by sending her to a farm where she could work — one of those work-camps the other two had told her about. Colette and Jeanne were glad of course, but could not help hiding their sadness. Lydia had become not only the symbol of the child each had always wanted, but she had become their close friend. The cell would not be the same without her. All three cried in chorus the night before the parting.

'Don't forget my address, Lydia, *chérie*,' said Jeanne. 'Look me up after the war and we'll paint Paris red, eh? We'll show them what a real party is like. And mind you eat well in the country. Lots of butter and lots of eggs and red wine. Ah, *merde*, I've forgotten what butter tastes like. But it'll fatten you up a bit.'

Colette took Lydia in her arms. 'Listen my child,' she said with a gravity in her voice that Lydia had never heard before. 'Listen carefully. When the war is over and we are all out of this dump and back in a place you can call home, we'll get together for — for a big slap-up meal at my place and we'll talk over the old times, the good old times we've had together. But listen. I know that here, well, here in this cell where we're all equals as it were, we don't mind each other. We have even grown to love each other, Jeanne, you and me. But when it's all over and we go back to our homes and our work, well, things may be a little different. You and I — well, we won't be equals any longer. D'you see what I'm trying to say? I mean — well, I'll have to go back to my old trade. It's the only thing I know how to do. It's the only thing I'm any good at.

'Now you — you'll become a great dancer. Oh, yes, I know you will. Both Jeanne and I know it. You'll be a great dancer and everyone will talk about you and you'll have your name in the papers and your picture will be there for all to see. But me... well, I'll just be a prostitute. Yes, darling, that's what I shall be, a prostitute, a *putain*, a *fille de joie*, a *traineuse*. The only good that men will be talking about me is if I've satisfied their lust, if I've given them their money's worth. And when you grow old and have to retire, you'll go somewhere in the country, and all the journalists will still follow you about and write long articles about the famous Lydia who now lives in quiet seclusion with her admirers.

'But me when I retire it'll be because no one comes to me any more for their franc's worth of love. It'll be because they've found some other fourteen-year-old kid who is pretty and who knows how to behave herself in bed. And I'll just grow old and wither and die in some gutter. And the police records will be able to strike off one more dirty name.

'So, darling Lydia, when you come to see me after the war, don't — don't think too badly of me. If my cheeks are painted a bit and I smear on too much powder and lipstick, don't hold it against me, will you? It'll only mean that without that powder and without that lipstick I shan't look pretty enough for the men who have made me what I am. Remember your old Colette and thank God you're not like her, Lydia my pretty, pretty sweet.'

CHAPTER TEN:

THE JOURNEY OF FEAR

Romainville was certainly in the country. It was a massive fortress used as a prison for political prisoners. For Lydia it was merely a question of being moved from one cage to another. And yet, as soon as she entered Romainville, she felt that she was going to be happy there. The sun was shining, the windows were larger, even if the bars were just as strong as anywhere else, and they were at a normal level. Greatest joy of all — Romainville was for both men and women. There was no mixing the two sexes; not even the French quisling guards would have been as broad minded as that. But, from the windows of the women's section, one could see quite plainly the men's block some fifty yards away.

Lydia was growing up. She was eighteen now, and a very beautiful eighteen at that, even if her cheeks lacked the rosiness of fresh air and youth and her lips were dry and pale. Her body had developed as best it could in the circumstances. Tuberculosis, even though a mild attack, did not help matters. Lydia was thinner than she should have been and her breasts made desperate attempts to remain firm and pointed defiantly against the thin material of her prison uniform. Her eyes still beamed with happiness should the sun throw its warming rays into her cell and gleamed sadness should the clouds erase the warmth of spring. She could speak with her eyes. They showed she was still alive in every sense of the word. And when she saw the men in the opposite compound, her eyes reflected the awakening passions of her heart. Men. Lydia had never thought of them properly. To her they represented partners for ballets or messengers for the Underground Movement. She had

had boy friends of sorts, but they had rather been comrades, friends who bought her the odd coffee or vin rouge, who had placed affectionate arms round her shoulders without their touch giving her any more sensation than a slight warmth or strength. Lydia had not really awakened sexually. She had not pined for anyone other than her father, mother and brother. She had, in fact, had no real adolescence Her childhood had been a fairly happy one as childhoods go, though her teenage stage had been totally missed. She had jumped from being a child to becoming a woman without experiencing the normal transgression steps. Love, other than parental love, was unknown to her. Colette and Jeanne had awakened her mind to the existence of men without awakening her heart. She had listened to their experiences of love-making in bewildered wonder. In these matters she was still a child and her understanding of sexual intimacies was totally blind.

But now, having heard of sex without having tasted it, she looked at men in a different light. The prisoners in the other block took on new shapes. They were no longer dancing partners and messengers. They awoke in Lydia sentiments she had never before experienced — passion. One of the prisoners stood out above all the others. He was a young man, handsome in a rugged, almost ugly kind of way. Broad shouldered and tall, he could swing a neat sledge hammer at the rocks the prisoners had to break up. Lydia could see the sun reflecting from his sweat, could almost smell his body — or imagined that she could. If only she could touch him, have him near her if only she could do with him what Collette had told her about. She was sure he would make a wonderful lover and an even better husband. Lydia suddenly realized that she was in love.

It must have been love. Whenever she saw him — and it was daily — she felt her heart beats grow faster. Her pulse pounded against every fibre of her body. Her lips grew moist and warm and her breathing quickened. Her hands gripped the bars of her open window until they were white with the strain. She wanted to shout to him, hear his voice, know his name. But she could do none of these things. Silence was one of the rules at Romainville and fraternization was not permitted under any circumstances. Lydia realized that it was crueler to be able to see men from a distance and not communicate with them, than it was to be alone in a dark, solitary cell away from everyone.

Every day she looked out for her nameless lover and every day her desire for him grew stronger. It was on one of these days, when the sun was shining particularly strongly and Lydia was looking out of her window that she had the surprise of her life. At first she could not believe it at all. A man, walking in the distance and against the strong sun, looked familiar. A small man, bent double under the weight of a log of wood he was carrying upon his shoulders, a thin man, weary and walking so slowly. Lydia rubbed her eyes, smarting from the glare. The little man walked a little closer —but the distance dividing her from him was still too great to be sure. Lydia held her breath as though the silence might help her hear her recognition.

'Papa!' It was a choked cry that left Lydia's lips. Her throat parched and tight found no power to shout the word any louder. It escaped her as a whimpering whisper mingled with tears. Her second attempt was only a little better. 'Pa-pa!' But her father had gone, his body blending with the grey-brown tones of the buildings in the men's compound.

All night Lydia lay in a fever. Had she made a mistake? Perhaps the sun had made her see some ghost. It was possibly just a strange hallucination. Perhaps the man she thought was her father had been someone else, someone who looked like him. After all, the distance, the light, these things were joined against her.

And yet and yet the man she had seen did look like her father, like some spirit of her father. She prayed to God that He might let her see this spirit again, that she might be quite sure that what she thought she had seen was indeed what she had seen.

'Forgive me, oh God, if I have turned my thought to other things — things that perhaps have not pleased You. Forgive me if I allowed my emotions to get the better of me that I even forgot about my family. It has been so long, dear God, so very long since I have seen any of them that I have forgotten what they even look like. Please, please let me see that man again — and God: let it be my father.'

Her prayer was answered two days later. And this time there was no mistaking him. Wladimir de Lipski was certainly thinner and had grown balder and looked weaker than she had ever seen him — but it was the same man who had helped bring her into the world. She shouted his name through the bars, the tears blinding her, drowning her — but he did not hear. The shadow of her father passed on into the distance and disappeared from view.

Now Lydia saw him almost every day. But he did not see her. It was just over a fortnight before the 'family reunion' took place.

And what a reunion it was! De Lipski spotted Lydia from a distance. He had already been told about her — not about Lydia his daughter, but of a girl who was constantly waving to him.

A young man whose name was Jean had managed to whisper a few words to him. It appeared this young man was in love with a girl in the women's compound though he did not even know who she was or what her name was.

Yet he had seen her often and, at first, had thought she was waving to him. But, on closer observation, he saw it was to the old man she was waving. The young man was puzzled. Admittedly, the 'old' man was not really so old, but he was certainly no sight for a young girl's heart. Jean whispered the information little by little to Lipski. And so it was that Lydia's father spotted her. And from a distance of some fifty yards, without any word being spoken, the reunion was accomplished and father and daughter managed to wave to each other.

It was a wave that spanned three years of separation.

It was a wave of victory, of joy, of life.

It was a wave of love.

It was a wave that neither de Lipski nor Lydia ever forgot.

And Jean, whose name Lydia did not know and whom she loved had been the messenger that brought father and daughter together again.

At the shower baths Lydia and her father and Jean could indirectly meet. They never met physically but the little notes they wrote were as good as a clandestine rendezvous. When one is anywhere long enough, one manages to think of ways and means of surmounting the unsurmountable.

Jean who discovered the name of the beautiful girl from her father and was relieved to learn that there was still a chance for him in this fortress, left a note for Lydia in the showers. Although men and women were kept strictly apart from one another, there was one place that was used by both sexes — the showers. Once a week there were two shifts for the showers. One for the men. One for the women. And here the letters were hidden, pathetic little love letters, hopeless in their hope, poetic in their alertness.

'My dear Lydia,' read the first note that Lydia found from Jean. 'Please forgive me for writing to you. I see you constantly at your window and your father told me who you are. Please would you do me the honour of coming dancing with me as soon as this is all over. Yours Jean.'

'Dear Monsieur Jean: your words gave me much pleasure. I look forward very much to meeting you. Please give my love to my father and ask him to look after himself. I am feeling very well now I know him to be near and that he has a friend. Gratefully, Lydia.'

'Dearest Lydia. Please God it won't last much longer now. I am longing to take you out dancing and hold you in my arms. You look very beautiful and I only wish you were nearer. Your father and I send you all our love. Jean.'

'My dear Jean: You have no idea how much I look forward to receiving your letters. It makes me feel civilized again. I pray for you and Papa every night. God bless you both and keep you safe. Lydia.'

'My darling: How marvellous to see you waving to me the other day. You are the most beautiful woman I have ever seen. To think that you are here in the showers after me, washing your body in the same room I have. Please forgive me these words, but I cannot contain myself any longer. I love you so very much, Lydia, my darling. Please say you love me just a little. J.'

'The answer, my dearest Jean, is yes. Yes, I do love you. I am sure of it since I have never experienced such curious passions before. I think it must be love. God bless you and Papa. Lydia.'

'My child: Jean has shown me your notes and has told me of his love for you. He is a very nice young man and one of us. I am well. Do take care, darling. You look so pale — but then my eyes are not what they used to be. I kiss you fondly and pray for you. Papa.'

'Sweetest, most beautiful beloved: I dream of you every night and during the day I long for the time that my work takes me in line with your window so that I can see but a glimpse of you and your golden hair. It won't be long now before we are in each other's arms. My lips burn for your lips. A bientôt chérie. J.'

'I too dream of you, dearest Jean. Last night you came into my cell (in my dream that is) and I felt very embarrassed because it was so untidy and I could offer you nothing to eat or drink. I was so ashamed that I woke up. I wish now that I had not been ashamed and that the dream could have continued. Love, Lydia.'

'Oh, beloved! Your note has made my blood surge through my body all week long. The nights are the loneliest I have ever spent in my life. How I wish I could transform myself into something so small that I could come to you. How lucky are the flies in this camp that they can fly through the bars of your window and caress you. How I wish I were one of them! I send you passionate kisses and my heart. Jean.'

Every day, as the summer drew on, Lydia and Jean and Wladimir would manage that odd wave. Every day the love that Lydia felt for the young man in the male block grew stronger and her body ached with a pain she had never before experienced. Love hurts but it had never hurt as much as this. The unattainable, so far yet only fifty yards away, presented to this young French woman the most painful torture to date. She would lie awake at night visualizing the two of them together after the war, Jean and her. She would see herself walking along the Champs-Eylsées arm in arm with the most handsome man in the world.

All the other people along the broad avenue would be staring at them. And the girls would look at her in envy and at Jean they would stare with desire. And Lydia and Jean would return to their apartment, an apartment in the *Seizième*, in Neuilly perhaps no, no (Lydia dismissed the thought from her day-dream) not there! No, the apartment would be either in the Place Furstemberg or overlooking the Place des Vosges (they were Lydia's favourite little squares in Paris). Anyway, they would return to *their*, yes *their* apartment and make love. And make love. And make love. And make love. To hell with all the other women in the world and all the other men. To hell with food. Who wants food when one can have Jean and make love? Who wants? And there would be children. Lots and lots of children! And all the boys would look like Jean. And she, Lydia, would dance for him. Dance for him, her beloved one. She would dance for him naked for she had nothing to hide from him. And both would dance together enfolded in each other's nakedness where everything was fresh and clean and un-evil. And they would live happily. Oh, so happily. Laughter would be their song. And they would kiss on the banks of the Seine and watch the barges float slowly by and the music of accordions would drift across the water from the cafés as they danced naked under the bridges of Paris alone, alone.

Lydia had never given herself to any man. But now, alone in her cell, during the long lonely nights, she gave herself to Jean, gave herself to her dreams. For what else was there left for her but her dreams?

The women worked at Romainville, too. Lydia was not as lucky as most of the others. The majority of women were taken daily out into the fields to pick potatoes, dig trenches for irrigation and they were even able to sing while they worked. But Lydia was taken to the laundry three days a week to wash the clothes and linen for the prison. The steam and the heat made her whole body ache and her head swim. At times the fits of coughing she had become used to at the Santé and at Fresnes returned to her. On other days she was made to sew bags and sacks for the potatoes gathered by the other female prisoners. She met only few women, spoke to even fewer. Romainville was not quite as comforting as Fresnes had been. And there were no monthly parcels. The food was fair but unvariable. Yet, despite all this, Lydia was happy. She felt as though she was in a home together with her father and her lover — even though she could never speak to them other than by the little notes she was able to write and hide away in the showers.

Lydia believed that there could never be another war once this one was over. There could never be another prison cell, never any more want or hunger or frustration. These things could never be — not when two people loved each other so much as Jean and Lydia. But one day, Lydia's dreams, hopes and plans were shattered. A German guard came into her cell and ordered her to pack.

'Pack your things quick. You will be ready to move out of here within half an hour. Hurry.'

'Pack? Where are you taking me please,' asked Lydia, her heart beating heavily as her eyes pleaded an answer.

The guard smiled and nodded comfortingly. 'It's all right. Don't look so frightened. You are being sent away on a little holiday, that's all.'

'But, please, sir, I don't want to go away on a holiday. Really, I don't. I'm quite happy here.'

The German looked at Lydia in astonishment. '*Verdammt nochmal!* I've never heard such a thing. You are going on a holiday whether you like it or not. And don't answer me back. Now get packed and *basta*, that's the end of the matter.' And he stalked out of the cell and slammed the door behind him.

Holiday? Where could they be sending her? Lydia's thoughts traced a pattern round her mind. At any other time she would have welcomed the news. But now she ran to the window in the hope that she might see her father or Jean. But there was no one she knew, no one to whom she could shout her news. How could she possibly let Jean know they were to be parted? There was so little time. And pack? What was there to pack. A few rags that were called clothes amounted to a sack-skirt and a blouse of cotton and pyjamas, a tiny slab of soap and a few sheets of toilet paper which she used as notepaper for her love letters. And there were the love letters themselves. Jean's love letters. They were hidden under the mattress of her bed. She dare not pack them in case she was searched. Hastily she brought them out and read them as quickly as she could, swallowing back her tears. One by one, she crumpled up those precious letters and ate them. It was the only way of hiding them and keeping them at the same time.

Barely had she swallowed the last of the letters, when the door was flung open and she was ordered out. They marched her into the yard where she joined a large group of other women prisoners, most of whom she had never seen before. Together they were packed into trucks and driven away from Romainville — the fortress where Lydia had found love.

[119]

The journey was a short one. At least it seemed so. The truck was filled with political prisoners like Lydia — old women and young; fat and thin — all jabbering away, trying to make up for the time they lost in silence. It is strange that when women assemble together without ever having seen each other before, they are able to discuss at once the most intimate topics. When women prisoners get together, their language is of the crudest vulgarity imaginable. Lydia was unable to understand half the things she heard and was surprised at her ignorance. After all, she thought, these women were talking in French. They were her comrades, her sisters. Yet the language they spoke might just as easily have been Chinese. And so Lydia drew back still deeper in to her shell and looked out and back towards the fortress she had just left. Jean and her father were somewhere behind those walls, wondering probably where she was, where she was going, who she was going with and why she was going there. For all they knew she might be going to her death. But the German had said she was being sent on a holiday. Certainly all the others in the truck seemed happy enough.

'Where are we going please? Do you know?' Lydia asked the question timidly to the fat, smelly woman on her left. The woman turned to her and handed her a toothless grin.

'Holy Mother o' Jesus, how the bloody hell should I know? Why don't you ask those bastard *boches*?' she answered and Lydia noticed that the woman's breath stank. It stank of nothing in particular. It just stank of rottenness and decay. '*Merci, Madame,*' said Lydia politely and turned away.

'*Eh, crotte et merde alors,*' the woman laughed. 'How's that for a polite little primadonna? Oh, *merci, Madame,*' she mimicked Lydia and delighted in her chance to mock someone. 'D'you know where I think we're going, *ma petite poupée*? I think we're going to hell. To hell! D'you hear me, *poupée*? Hell! And d'you know what we shall find when we get there? I'll tell you what we'll find. We'll find a lot of them boche bastards there. They own the place. Yes, own the place, them bastards. They own every goddam thing in the whole goddam world. And you can be bloody certain that we'll be going there for just one good reason. To be stuffed by 'em. That's what we're going there for. Believe me, *ma petite poupée*, I've been stuffed by some funny fellows in my time but never by no bastard *boche* and I shan't let none of 'em touch me now neither. I'd first rot and let 'em tear my guts out before I'd let a single one of them sons o'bitches stuff me, I can tell you that much for free, I can. Not a one. Not a single goddam one... and she screeched a loud, long laugh that set the rest of the truck rocking with hysterical giggling. Even Lydia joined in but she felt embarrassed.

The trucks ground to a halt and their monotonous rumbling and the smell of petrol and oil was exchanged for the hiss of steam, the metallic clank of wheels on rails and the excited voices one normally hears at country stations. Soldiers helped the women down from the trucks and escorted them to the train standing nearest them. It was no more than a cattle train. But there were no cattle. The carriages were soon filled with their human cargo. The German soldiers were almost polite as they helped the passengers climb the steps into the long, wooden, stuffy carriages. An officer stood back, away from it all and eventually a sergeant approached him and saluted smartly.

'Tausend-fünfhundert fertig, mein Kommandant,' he announced in the guttural screech of the Prussian trained soldier.

'Gut. Lassen's abfahren,' replied the officer quietly. The news that there were indeed 1,500 women on that train had not come as news to him. He had been ordered to obtain 1,500 women and he had obtained them. He had even signed a form to that effect. He remembered signing similar forms when he was a junior director in his father's firm in Hamburg. They were shipping merchants. Yes, he thought, they had been just such forms. Only then he was signing for the receipt or shipment of radio sets or soap. This time it was women, French women. He ordered the sergeant to let the train go on its journey. 'The ship is loaded; let it sail.' No, there was no difference.

'Abfahren!' The sergeant screamed the order to the engine driver leaning out from his cabin. The sergeant used to be in charge of a section of a slaughter house in Wuppertal. He now looked at the women peering through the slits in the wooden carriages. All he could see was their eyes. All he could hear was their voices babbling away in French. Cattle did not make so much noise, he thought. Only when they were about to be executed did they give out high pitched wails. He did not understand the wailing of the cattle and he did not now understand the bleating women. No, he thought, there was not much difference really. The Fuehrer must be right. He must be right. These creatures whose eyes stared blindly through the slits were the enemies of the Fatherland. Good riddance, thought the sergeant.

The officer watched the train move slowly along the rails. Poor bastards, he thought. And, as the train chugged into the French countryside, he added half aloud: 'May God forgive me — for I know what I do.'

Inside the cattle trucks the women began to sing. They were the songs of their childhood, songs they used to sing when they went on school outings or on picnics with their parents. *'Frère Jacques', 'Au clair de la lune', 'Sur le Pont d'Avignon'....* But as the journey grew longer the women grew weary of singing. They were locked in. Almost two hundred women were crammed into each of the eight carriages. There was no room to lie down, hardly room to sit. During the day the sun added to the discomforting heat inside those moving cages.

At night it was cold. Bitterly cold. The women were glad to be so close together, begging for each other's warmth. Somewhere in the dark a girl cried. And her sobs soon found partners. Soon the whole train was weeping. It was like a long cortege at a funeral. Lydia, too, was crying. She cried for her beloved Jean, for her father. No one knew where they were going. But somehow all of them had come to the conclusion deep in their hearts that this was going to be no holiday.

An old woman at Lydia's side suddenly collapsed. Lydia had not even noticed her before now. 'Give her air,' a girl nearby shouted automatically as it was the thing to shout when someone faints. But there was no air to give since the women could not move out of the way easily. Lydia held on to the woman until there was space enough on the floor to allow her to sit. The old woman's eyes opened weakly in the darkness of the night. Her voice was hoarse and barely audible. 'Please — say — a — prayer for me,' she pleaded, clutching Lydia's arm with her own thin, bony fingers. 'I don't think I shall — arrive. Yet I feel — happy — not to arrive there.' Lydia, tears streaming down her cold cheeks, tried not to make her voice too shaky as she prayed. It was not one of the set prayers for she knew none for such an occasion. But nevertheless it was, she felt, the sort of prayer that God would understand.

'Dearest God,' she began and slowly the carriage became silent and the sobbing ceased as she continued. 'Look down upon this dear old woman, whose name I do not even know, and have mercy upon her. She is a good woman, I am sure, or else she would not be among us now. We are all sinners and yet we are all Your children and love You, God. This woman, too, loves You. She says she may not be able to make the long journey that lies ahead of us. If what she thinks is true, then at least, we beg of You, make her other journey a happy one. Give her peace, dear God. Give her everlasting peace and let her live in your Kingdom happily. For Your Kingdom is so much more happy than ours down here. You have created us what we are, God. It is up to You to give and to take away. If You take away this, your child, then it is probably because You think she has suffered enough. And if You believe that we who live on have not yet suffered enough, then we pray You, give us the courage, the strength and the will to endure our suffering in Your name and in the name of Our Lord Jesus Christ — Amen.' Two hundred voices echoed the Amen. And the journey continued.

In the morning the old woman was dead. But on her lips there was a smile of contentment. She was still lying in Lydia's arms, heavy and cold.

In other parts of the carriage, women were being sick. There were no facilities for any form of sanitation. And since there was also no room in which to move, they had to perform their natural functions more or less on the spot.

It was not long before the carriage transporting the women to an unknown destination stank. It reeked of urine, of excreta, of vomit, of death. Particularly of death. During the journey that lasted three days and two nights, four women died in Lydia's carriage alone. When they did so, those standing near to them called over to Lydia: 'Hey, say another prayer. For God's sake say another prayer.' And Lydia, tired and sick herself, spoke other prayers. Her prayers brought courage to the rest of those women. Courage and comfort.

During the warm, sunny days, as the train passed slowly through the French countryside, stopping from time to time, the women peered out through the slits and waved to peasants working in the fields. 'How about some food?' the women called, for no one had eaten since the journey began. But the peasants scowled back and remained where they were. No one came close to the train. No one offered so much as a raw potato. And some of the farmers even shook their fists at the women. Strange, thought Lydia, that people could change so very much in so comparatively short a time. Why were they so unfriendly, these French farmers? Did they not realize the hunger, the thirst, the discomfort that existed in those cattle trucks? The women in the carriages cursed the peasants but were much too weak to let their curses be heard. Only their cries for water and food did they project across the fields. But no one answered them.

Slowly the scenery changed. Slowly, so slowly, did the train move along through different types of villages and small towns.

'Good God help us,' one of the women in Lydia's truck screamed as they were passing through a village. 'We're — we're in Germany!'

True enough, the language of the words painted outside shops was German. *'G. MÜLLER—KOLONIALWAREN' read one sign over a shop. 'FRIEDRICH SCHRÖDER UND SOHN—SPIELWAREN'* read another. And yet, considering the women had now come into the very laps of their enemies, the atmosphere was quite different from what they had experienced from their own compatriots in the fields of France. The Germans cheered them and threw them the hated Hitler salute. They waved and blew kisses. They even smiled. Lydia and the others could not understand this changed attitude. It was quite the opposite to what they should have expected. But there were no jeers, no shaking of fists, no curses.

Only later, when the train reached its destination was this curious attitude on the part of both French and Germans explained. On the outside of the train, painted in large white letters, hastily performed after the women had been ushered into their trucks, were the words (in French and German): 'Volunteer Workers for the German Reich.'

The train reached its destination at last. It ground to a halt. The women, what was left of them, were again put into a series of trucks and driven away.

The Germans dragged fifty-four corpses from the carriages. The manner in which they dragged them out showed that they were used to so grim a task.

The way they ordered the women into the trucks showed that they had been highly organized and experienced in handing out orders. They punched away at those older females who were unable to move quite quickly enough for their liking. They kicked at those who collapsed to the ground, then lifted them up and threw them like sacks of potatoes into the trucks. They seemed to enjoy their job, even though their faces did not betray it. Indeed, their faces wore the expressions of bestiality. One would never have believed that these men who kicked old women in the breast were the sons of the same nation that had created Goethe and Schiller, Beethoven and Wagner, Kant and Schopenhauer. Nor would one have believed that they had been different before the appearance of Adolf Hitler ten years earlier. Had it only taken one decade, one minute breath of history, to transform cultured human beings into cruel beasts without brain, without feeling? It all seemed so incredible.

The journey by truck took about twenty-five minutes. Lydia heard some gates open and shut again behind them as the trucks entered what she supposed to be her next prison. They had arrived at their holiday camp. It was to be quite a holiday. For the name of the camp was Ravensbrück.

CHAPTER ELEVEN:

NIGHT, FOG AND RAVENSBRÜCK

Ravensbrück. Sometimes the inmates called it 'Grabensbrück' or the Bridge of Graves. For that is exactly what it was: a graveyard. A living graveyard. At first Lydia could not believe the things that she saw. The whole thing was like a nightmare. She sincerely believed at first that she had also died on that long train journey and that she had arrived in hell. Surely, she thought, all these people could not be human beings. Eyes were staring at the new arrivals. Eyes that were large and terrifyingly sad. Expressionless eyes in hollow sockets, carved into faces that did not exist. The people she saw, if they were indeed people, were so meagre, their bones could be seen clearly through their paper-thin garments.

Lydia was eighteen. She had not yet experienced the passions of love; she had almost forgotten the meaning of the word 'freedom': she had already spent three years in three French prisons for her crime of helping her father and some two hundred others spy for England against the Nazi invaders of her homeland. But those French prisons had been like so many children's playgrounds compared to this camp of the living dead.

She wanted to scream, turn and run. But her throat was dry and tight with fear and horror and her legs felt as though they had been anchored down with lead. Her companions, like her, were too overcome by such utter despair that they marched slowly and in silence towards the commandant's office.

Lydia looked about her. A brown building to her right and some four hundred yards away had a large chimney. Black smoke belched from it. Perhaps that is where the kitchens are, thought Lydia. Perhaps they would be serving some sort of food soon.... She did not know that this building was the camp crematorium and that the smoke she saw was the result of burning bodies. Nor did she know that many of those bodies being burned were still alive when they went to the flames.

Barbed wire surrounded the camp. There were two layers of this wire. It should not be too difficult to crawl under it and escape, thought Lydia. She did not know that the wire was highly electrified. Nor did she know that those women who had tried to escape had been instantly killed by the electric shock. She did not even know that many women had deliberately flung themselves against the wire, embracing death as they would a liberator. For it was easier to die at Ravensbrück than to live there.

The long line of new arrivals was ordered to halt and was then arranged in five rows. Thus they were ordered to stand and wait.

'One word out of you, any of you, and the talker will be shot,' was the command from a soldier. He wore the uniform of the S.S. and could not have been more than twenty years old.

They stood there, cold, hungry and sick, not daring to turn round to look at the coldness, the hunger and the sickness around them. For two hours they stood there, each thinking her thoughts, each praying her prayers. Behind them they could hear the wails of women. Languages they had not heard before were being spoken. German orders were barked. They heard a shot and more wailing. Death hung in the air. And the chimney continued to issue smoke that formed a sooty screen over the camp.

Lydia thought of her father and Jean back at Romainville. How lucky they were to be in a French fortress. 'Please dear God, let them stay there until all this ghastly thing is over,' prayed Lydia silently. 'And let them never know the circumstances of my death.' For she was convinced she had come here to die. How could one live in such misery, such terror and survive? It could not be done, thought Lydia. But she decided that whatever happened, she would remain calm and, if God willed, she would remain courageous to the end. This vow she made to herself while standing in the cold dusk of Ravensbrück.

The camp commandant arrived. He introduced himself. 'My name is Hubert Schwatz* and I am in charge of this camp,' were his opening words. They were spoken in German and translated by an interpreter into French. Schwatz was a fat little man, with beady pig-eyes and an almost completely bald head. Lydia felt sick merely looking at him.

---

*Schwatz was sentenced to death by hanging at the Nuremberg War Crimes trials.

'You are in Germany now and the fun and games of France are over,' he continued, rasping out each word as though it was dirty and he wished to be rid of it quickly. Fun and games indeed, thought Lydia. Who the hell does he think he is? 'You will be taken to various huts here in the camp,' Schwatz went on. 'These huts should be treated like your own home and are to be kept spotlessly clean — though I'm sure that most of you don't even know what that word means. You have all been brought up in a country where people urinate freely in the streets. But this is Germany and here we do not urinate in the street. Here we are clean and I am going to try and teach you how to be clean too.' While the interpreter — a blond German youth who might have been attractive had it not been for his cruel mouth — was translating the commandant's words in fairly fluent but badly accented French, Schwatz looked sneeringly round the parade of women before him. He hated every one of them. His eyes met Lydia's and he looked her up and down appraising her value as a woman. He gave a careful scrutiny of every young girl in the consignment.

'You may find it a little crowded here sometimes,' he said now. 'I wish to hear no complaints from any of you. I have my hands full enough as it is. If any of you are sick, there is an excellent hospital here and doctors who will take care of you — though God knows none of you is worth being taken care of. I shall now have your names read from a list and I want you to answer your name loud and clear.'

The roll-call was made. It took an eternity. An S.S. soldier read the long list slowly and loudly. 'Arles, Jeanne,' he began. A voice somewhere in the crowd replied weakly, 'Here.' 'What? What was that? I ordered you to shout up loud and clear,' the commandant interrupted. 'I can hear the name but I hear no reply. Say again — and it had better be loud this time.'

'Arles, Jeanne,' the soldier repeated.

'Here,' came the reply, still weak but much louder and quite audible.

'Brunell, Alice.'

'Stop! *Zum donnerwetter nochmal* where the hell do you all think you are? In a holiday camp?' The commandant was very angry indeed and stamped his foot in temper. 'When you answer, you will not just say "here". You will call out "Here, sir." "Here, sir!" Is that understood? From now on, you will call every German official in this camp "Sir" and I am Herr Kommandant. Show some respect you dirty lot of pigs. Pah, pfui! Now continue.'

'Brunell, Alice…'

'No, no, no, *Unteroffizier Benz*,' Schwatz called and stamped his foot again. 'Start from the beginning. I have not yet heard a correct reply from that — that person whose name you called first.' And answer him correctly this time, d'you hear, you stupid, ignorant little whore...'

'Arles, Jeanne,' the soldier called.

'Here, sir,' came the reply.

'Brunell, Alice,'

'Here, sir.'

'Buber, Constance.'

'Here, sir.'

'Buronne, Francoise.'

There was no reply and the name was repeated twice. There was still no reply. The commandant shouted: 'Well, where the devil is she? Bu-ronne? Who knows where this bitch is?'

A voice from the third row replied with a scream: 'You stupid bastard, don't you know? You damn well ought to know, damn you. You murdered her Yes, you little swine. You and your stupid Fuehrer's henchmen. You murdered her. She died on that shitting contraption you called a train. And she was my mother blast you, my mother!' While she was screaming, soldiers ran through the rows of women to grab her. Meanwhile Schwatz was growing livid with rage and his face contracted in the dusk while his fists clenched and he stamped his foot hysterically on the platform on which he was standing. 'Stop her! Stop her at once.' But before the soldiers reached her, Agnes Buronne was able to add a few words. 'I curse you Schwatz and I curse all your family. May you all rot in hell and Hitler along with you!'

At that point one of the soldiers had reached her and clubbed her over the head with his revolver.

'Soll ich sie erschiessen Herr Kommandant?' he called to Schwatz and pointed the revolver down at the woman's head, ready and willing to shoot her there where she lay. The soldier looked disappointed when Schwatz refused his offer to shoot her on the spot.

'No,' said Schwatz and his breathing was heavy. 'She is not worth a bullet. But she will join her precious mother soon enough. By God, I shall make her suffer for what she has just said. Now listen all of you. That woman who lies there is a traitor and a witch. I shall make an example of her to show you exactly what you can expect if you start behaving in that sort of way. I am used to you filthy swine. I'll show you. I'll show the lot of you!'

They dragged Agnes Buronne away into Schwatz's office, limp and bleeding from where the revolver had struck her head. And the roll call continued.

After the roll call was completed, the consignment of Frenchwomen was divided up into groups and assigned to their billets. Because Lydia had been

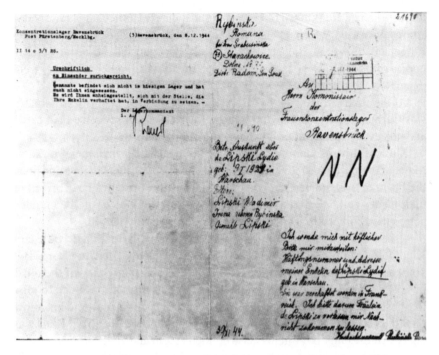

13. This is a facsimile of the letter to the Camp Commandant of Ravensbrück by Lydia's grandmother, Madame Romana Rydinska in Poland. 'I turn to you and beg you most kindly to let me know: the prison number and address of my granddaughter de Lipski, Lydia, born in Warsaw. She was arrested in France. I sincerely ask you to allow Fräulein de Lipski to send me news of her.'

The letter, which was date-stamped 7 December 1944 was also marked N.N. (Nacht und Nebel) by the Camp authorities. The letter itself was dated 30 November 1944. A week later the Camp Commandant's assistant wrote this reply:

'Returned to sender. This person is not in this camp and has never been in it. You are informed to contact the place which arrested your granddaughter.'

in the Resistance she was placed into N.N. Block 32.

N.N. was the abbreviation for *Nacht und Nebel*—Night and Fog. N.N. stood for certain death and all the prisoners placed in to this section were on the black list. They were never to return to their homes, never to see their loved ones again.

It was a foregone conclusion that Lydia would one day be dragged off to the ever burning crematorium to be turned into ashes. It was at Ravensbrück that prisoners were skinned like animals and their skin turned into lampshades and canvases on which to paint the delightful landscapes of the German Rhineland. It was at Ravensbrück that the fat collected from the burning bodies of prisoners was used to make soap with which other prisoners were made to wash themselves.

At the time Lydia came to this 'holiday camp', the majority of inmates was German, Polish, Dutch and Czech. They were treated worse than cattle and had every vestige of pride knocked out of them.

Most of the prisoners were there for political rather than racial reasons. Many of them were Catholics, many others had defied orders to love and obey the Fuehrer. And the Fuehrer had ordered that these creatures be deprived of their names and be given a number instead. This number was to be branded across their foreheads. This was one order that was not obeyed.

'I had a son once,' one middle-aged German woman called Hildegard Kindl told Lydia shortly after her arrival. 'He was a good lad, my Hans. But you know what it is with children. They like to be exactly like all the other boys and when it came to joining the Hitler Youth, Hans also wanted to join. My husband, Karl — ach, God knows where he is, poor man — did not allow him to do so and I was entirely of the same opinion, you see. Well, Hans was angry. All the other boys in his class pointed at him and called him names for not being one of them, and he, of course, blamed us for this. So eventually we said all right, go ahead and join but don't believe everything you are told. We are still your parents, we said, and we are the ones who love you. D'you think he listened? No. He actually told the Gruppenfuehrer that my husband and I had listened to a foreign radio station and that we were against Hitler. So we were both arrested.

'And my little Hans, d'you know where he was when they came for us? He stood right outside the door and when we passed him, he threw up his hand in a Nazi salute and shouted Heil Hitler and said "that'll serve you right." I'll never forget his words till the day I die. Karl is somewhere else. I think they took him to Dachau, but I'm not sure. He was a good boy, though, was Hans before they got hold of him.'

'How old is he?' asked Lydia.

'He'll be fifteen next November. Yes, on November 22nd he'll be fifteen. I hope he'll grow up and come to his senses, that's all. I still say a prayer for him.' And Frau Kindl looked up at Lydia and, clutching her gently by the arm, said: 'You must not think that all Germans are bad. It's just you see, that so many have gone mad, have been hypnotized by a maniac. They have forgotten even their own parents. I am sorry you are here. You are so pretty and so young. *Ach, du lieber guter Gott, wo soll das noch alles enden?'*

'Here you! Here's your number.'

Lydia was handed her number. It was 21690. And there was also a red triangle which she had to sew on alongside the number. The red triangle signified that Lydia Lipski was a political prisoner. German Gypsies were given black triangles and those with 'other reasons' for being at the camp wore green triangles. These so-called *'andere Gründe'* included criminals, thieves and lesbians. Jews had not yet been sent to Ravensbrück. They had been herded into other camps, camps like Auschwitz, Bergen-Belsen, Dachau, camps where more than one crematorium burned day and night, where gas chambers were ever-busy.

Block 32 N.N. This was home. A shed measuring fourteen by five metres. In it were five hundred bunks. And in those five hundred bunks 'lived' one thousand women.

The stink in that shed was unbelievable. It was like a hundred public lavatories put together and not cleaned for a year. As soon as Lydia entered she felt dizzy and vomited.

'Clean that mess up at once,' the guard who had accompanied her and twenty others from her group ordered, turning his face away. *'So eine Schweinerei.'* Lydia cleaned up the mess with a piece of rag another woman had handed her. The rag smelled as though it had been used exclusively for this purpose. There was not very much mess really, for Lydia had not eaten for nearly four days. Her stomach was empty and what there was to wipe up was merely bile.

She looked about her. The crawling remains of human beings met her eyes. Sunken cheeks, large eyes, flabby breasts, motionless, lifeless yet living.

'Where do you come from then, my pretty, eh?' Lydia turned round. At her side, stroking her arm was a woman of thirty or thirty-five, well made and better nourished than the others. 'My name is Lise, what's yours?'

'Lydia,' said Lydia, drawing her arm away instinctively.

'Well, Lydia, you and I should get on rather well, I think. I could get you some food if you're hungry. Are you hungry, darling?'

Well, yes I am — but....' There was something about the woman, something new and strange to Lydia. Lise spoke to her in French but it was the somewhat guttural French of Alsace rather than that of France and there was something feline in her manner. Her speech purred out of her mouth and her eyes shone with a green sparkle that Lydia had not expected to find among these human skeletons.

'Then I shall be right back with something to eat. You see, I'm rather —

er — friendly with the cook.'

And Lise disappeared. Lydia stood there not knowing whether to laugh at this tragi-comic situation or to cry. Another woman approached Lydia and said: 'Look kid, I don't know whether you know about such things or not, but that girl is not the best kind to kip up with. She'll devour you whole, she will. I should leave well alone if I were you. What's more, she also sleeps with one of the German guards.'

'You mean she sleeps with the guard and the cook?' asked Lydia. 'Then that explains why she looks so much better than the rest.'

'Yes, correct. Only it's even funnier than that. You may not have realized it yet, but you see, the cook — or at least the cook she sleeps with happens to be a woman and the guard is, of course, a man. So she has the best of both worlds. She is what one might call ambisextrous.'

Lesbianism could hardly be avoided at Ravensbrück. When one thousand women have to share five hundred bunks (placed alongside the walls of the hut in tiers of three) in the bitter cold of winter or the oppressing heat of summer, in hunger and in misery, such relationships become normal. The women slept — if, indeed, they were at all able to sleep — mostly head to foot. Clothes were thin and ragged. The only bedding consisted of a flimsy cotton sheet shared between two. The Germans called them blankets. This, too, was normal. For even a cold, hard potato was considered a meal fit for a king.

Lydia moved along the line of bunks searching for one that was free.

'*Eh, voilà, ma petite.* You are French, are you not?'

Lydia looked around for the voice's owner. She saw a thin woman of some sixty years beckoning to her. After what she had just been told regarding Lesbianism, she looked at everyone and everything in a different light — the light of fear of the unknown. But this woman, she could see, was elderly and, despite her ragged clothes and her thin grey hair, her sunken cheeks and slightly trembling hands, looked like a lady of some importance. Lydia approached her slowly, shyly. 'What is your name, my child?' asked the woman. And she smiled kindly at Lydia. It was a smile of compassion, of welcome and put the young girl at her ease for the first time since she had arrived at the camp.

'Lydia, Madame. Lydia de Korczac Lipski.' Lydia rarely gave her full aristocratic name and yet, on this occasion, could not resist it.

'A good name,' said the woman. 'A name of which you may be justly proud I am sure. And the way you pronounced it makes me, too, feel proud that there are still young women left who know how to value their names.

May I introduce myself. I am the Countess de Ganay.'

The old woman held her head up high as she told Lydia her own name and the rags she wore turned into the silks and satins of a princess. Her grey hair shone like a crown and her trembling hands took on a firmness conjured up by supreme will-power.

'I am deeply honoured to make your acquaintance, Madame,' said Lydia and curtsied low. Such a scene would normally have caused laughter and scorn in any other circumstances, but the prisoners who witnessed this strange ritual in that den of death did not laugh. Those few who were still able to think at all philosophically did not even find the scene pathetic. Instead, there was something beautiful, something very clean and gracious in the encounter between the old countess and the young daughter of a Polish prince.

'My child, I am deeply touched by your politeness. There is so little of it left nowadays. So very little, alas. You will grow old here in a matter of minutes. You will hear things and see things that should never have been for your ears and eyes that should never have been for anyone ever to hear and see. But you must excuse the weakness of these people who are to be your companions. For they, too, have been thrown here through no fault of their own and because of what they have heard and seen have lost their sense of humanity and been weakened.'

Lydia listened to the speech in silence. Here spoke a wise old woman who, it was not difficult to see, had once been very beautiful and who had now aged far beyond her sixty years yet retained the pride of her House. Lydia had often heard her father speak of the Countess de Ganay and of the great work she had performed on behalf of the French Resistance. Lydia now told the countess this.

'Ah, dear me, I did not realize that I was so famous,' the old lady replied and laughed and her laughter tinkled like church bells through a fog. But Lydia detected a flush of pride rising in the lady's cheeks and was glad that she had been formal and friendly with her. The countess, ever concerned at keeping and practising the few last vestiges of etiquette, went on: 'But you honour me unnecessarily for what I did was merely my duty as a Frenchwoman and I carried it out to the best of my very poor ability. But you, my child, you did not need to do the things you did. Nor did your father. Le Prince de Korczac Lipski, even if he was French by naturalization, was still Polish by heart. He did not really have to fight for France. His duty lay, if anywhere, in Poland. But he decided most gallantly to aid my dear, poor little country. You look surprised, my child. Oh, yes, your father's name is not unknown to me. Nor for that matter is yours. Indeed, I know even the very circumstances of how you were betrayed. But do not worry. That woman (and she referred to Micheline Carré) will pay for her crime. France never forgets those who have sinned against her or those who have come to her aid.'

Lydia and the Countess de Ganay became close friends. The old countess was like a mother to the young girl and taught her how to keep up her morale.

'The only way to survive in this terrible place is to keep one's morale,' she said. 'And the only way to keep one's morale is to keep one's body and one's mind clean. This is not easy. Most of the people here have forgotten that they are God's children. Most of them have forgotten they are human beings. They have become animals. The Germans have very successfully turned good, honest people into thieves. They have transformed cleanliness into the dirtiest filth imaginable. They have changed good women into prostitutes and have brought about corruption and vice out of honesty. There is only one way to conquer the Germans in this camp, my dear. And that is to keep yourself thoroughly clean. Wash whenever you can. And pray. Prayer is needed here for when the devil is all about you, seeking a way to rob you of your soul, then only your nearness to God can help. I was never a good Christian. Yet now, my child, I feel myself at one with my Maker. It is necessary. So very necessary.'

Lydia shared the bunk with the Countess de Ganay, sleeping with her head at the countess' feet and feeling ashamed and embarrassed that this great old lady should have to endure the same indignity as her.

It was not difficult to see how quickly the good women the countess spoke of were turned into beasts. Almost as soon as the new consignment had arrived at Ravensbrück and the party had been allocated to N.N. Block 32, there were fights. Fights over crusts of bread. Fights over where to sleep and who would sleep with whom.

The best bunks were considered to be those at the top of the tiers. The reason was simple. Since there was still a little space left between the top bunk and the roof of the hut, it was easier to breathe than it was in either of the two remaining bunks below. It was also safer up there. Many women were sick during the night. If one slept on one of the lower bunks and the prisoner above was sick, the girl below was apt to receive the worst of it. As soon as a girl in a top bunk died — and deaths were many and frequent — those below and alongside would fight for the right to take over. These fights would occur even before the corpse had been removed to the crematorium and was still lying warm on the hard boards called a bed.

The Polish prisoners were by far the most expert thieves at Ravensbrück. It was not a case of always having been a thief. On the contrary, many of the Poles at the camp had come to it as honest citizens whose only crime had been to fight the Germans in an attempt to liberate their country of the conquering jackboot. But once inside, the Poles were quick to adapt themselves to a life of fighting for survival.

One of the Polish girls in Lydia's hut somehow managed to obtain a little saw. Where she had obtained it was always a mystery, but she made excellent use of it. Each night she would cut into the roof of her lower bunk after the girls were asleep. Soon she had cut a hole large enough to put her hand through and, without disturbing the girl above, stole all her little valuables from under her pillow.

All the prisoners kept what little treasures they had under their pillow — which was, in fact, no more than a piece of sacking around wood shavings which added to the discomfort of an already hard wooden bunk. The treasures included the little slab of coarse soap that was distributed once a month to the prisoners, a crust of bread or some other morsel of food which the enterprising prisoner may have managed to 'organize' from the kitchen or which may have been given her as a bribe for allowing other prisoners to make love to her. Other precious items included bits of combs, mostly 'home-made' from pieces of wood found outside. Normally a prisoner would have to defend with her life any food she had. She would first hide it under her thin grey uniform, in the pit of her arm or in other parts of the body, and then transfer it under her pillow. She would nibble at a crust of bread for days. It was luxury.

During the two years Lydia spent at the camp, she tried always to keep the advice given her by the countess, and kept herself as clean as was possible in the circumstances. Reveille was at 3 a.m. and at that time there was a stampede for the washbasins outside. There were only twenty basins for a thousand women — and two lavatories of the country type, a wooden seat over a deep pit. Most of the women were unable to wash at all. They were too slow and they only had a few minutes to complete the exercise before having to line up for roll call. So Lydia would wake up at 2.30 in the morning and make her way silently to the basins to wash herself thoroughly. The countess normally went with her at this time.

The clamour of a thousand women around twenty basins was chaotic. There were screams and yells as one would tear at the other for the right to wash. Fights. Always there were fights. The women fought for everything at all hours of the day. They even fought for the right to clean out the lavatory pits, for although this was by far one of the most distressing jobs in the camp, during the winter it was one of the warmest. Those pits stank. But at least they were warm and one was able to take one's time cleaning them out, resting and keeping the circulation going.

CHAPTER TWELVE:
THOSE WHO TRESPASSED...

Block 32, like all the others in the camp, had a hut leader. This was normally the prettiest girl in the hut. She was personally picked and favoured by the Block Commandant — a woman. In the case of Block 32, the girl chosen as leader was Lise Schaefer, the girl who had first 'welcomed' Lydia. Lise was a girl of many parts. She slept with one of the guards, with one of the cooks and with the Block Commandant — a young woman named Binz.

And Fräulein Binz was, at twenty-four, probably the cruelest woman in the camp. Blonde and attractive, she was never without her whip. This she used freely and with much pleasure on young and old alike. The Camp Commandant had given her complete liberty as to how to manage her prisoners — and she used that liberty to the fullest extent and without shame.

Shortly after Lydia's arrival, Fraulein Binz called her to her office. It was Lise who brought the message.

'Fraulein Binz wants you Lydia darling,' she cooed, eyes blazing. 'I need hardly tell you that she has quite a soft spot for you.'

'What on earth do you mean — a soft spot?'

'Well, you see, I told her about you. Told her that you were not like the others, that you were, well, shall we say, pretty? I hope that you will remember me after you have seen her and be a little friendlier than you have been before. After all, you and I could get on splendidly together, now couldn't we? So if you're nice to Binzlein, she'll be nice to you. And then things could be a lot easier all round. Don't you agree?'

'I don't know what you mean by being nice to her, but I'm willing to go along and see what she has to say,' said Lydia on her guard.

Lydia went and knocked at the Block Commandant's door.

'Herein!' The voice was harsh, unfriendly, chilled with cruelty. Lydia went in and shut the door behind her. Binz was sitting behind her desk smoking a short cheroot. She looked up at Lydia and ordered her to come nearer and stand before the desk. Lydia did so. She dared hardly look at the woman behind the desk but could feel herself being devoured by her eyes. The silence seemed interminable. At last Binz finished her slow, meticulous inspection of Lydia, stood up and came round to the front of the desk, sat on the edge of it and crossed her shapely legs.

'You're an extremely lovely girl, d'you know that?' she said in a matter-of-fact tone. Lydia said nothing.

Binz went on. 'If you like, I can put you in the kitchens to work. It's clean there and you'll be able to eat plenty. I'm not all that bad, you know. I don't really like seeing all you young girls going around cold and hungry and half naked. When did you last sleep with a man?' The question came like a bolt of lightning and Lydia blushed deep red. 'Well, when?'

'I — I've never slept with any man, ma'am,' Lydia stammered and dropped her eyes upon the ground in utter embarrassment. 'What! Never? Not once?'

'N — no, ma'am.'

Binz smiled triumphantly. This was indeed a rich morsel. 'Strip off,' she ordered.

'I — I beg your pardon?'

'You heard me. Take your clothes off, blast you. That's an order. I'm not going to bite you. Just want to look at you.'

Lydia did as she was told and Binz gazed at the girl with a mixture of total admiration and desire. She threw the end of her cheroot onto the ground, stood up, stamped on it and came over to Lydia. For a moment she stood very close to the young girl, studying her face, neck and breasts. Then suddenly she threw her arms around Lydia and kissed her full on the lips. Lydia uttered a muffled scream and struggled free.

'Damn you, damn you, who do you think you are? And who do you think I am?' Lydia screamed, beetroot red with shame and anger. 'Just because you have been given a lot of helpless women to look after does not give you the right to buy their souls or their bodies. I am French and if ever I allow anyone to make love to me it is going to be the man I love and not some — some creature like you. You cannot buy me. I'd rather you kill me first.'

[137]

Binz listened to this harangue in amazement. She had never been pushed off like this before. No one had ever dared. Now this slip of a girl had actually insulted her as though — as though she were a common whore. She, a good, pure Aryan would not stand such insults from a French hussy.

'By God and by the name of the Fuehrer, you shall pay for this outburst, you little bitch, you,' she shouted at Lydia. 'Kill you first, eh? Right, you've asked for it.'

Binz was in a raging temper now. The sweat stood out on her brow and the knuckles of her clenched fists showed white. She grabbed her whip and lashed out at Lydia. She struck blow after blow until Lydia lay bleeding and unconscious on the ground. Binz followed up her whipping with kicks and when she had worked off her rage, spat upon the still form lying on the floor. Binz then strode over to the door, opened it and called: 'Schaefer! Schaefer, come here.'

Lise came trotting up at the double. 'What is it, Fraulein Binz? What's the matter?'

'Get this — this thing out of here,' Binz said quietly but breathing heavily. 'Get her out — and don't let me see her again. If I do, so help me I'll whip her to death. The little scum, the little bitch.

Lise dragged Lydia naked back to the hut and put her on her bunk. 'You fool, Lydia, you silly, silly fool. What did you do? What could you have said to her? Things could have been so good, so easy for you. Oh, you silly little fool.'

The Countess de Ganay nursed Lydia back to health, washed her wounds in water and her own tears. And when Lydia had recovered sufficiently to sit up, the countess wound her arms around her. *'Ma petite, ma pauvre, brave petite,'* she cooed, rocking Lydia in her arms. 'You are indeed a Korczac Lipski. A brave girl. They won't kill you in such a hurry. You showed strength and great courage. But now you must show even greater courage, for your life here will be harder than for any of us.'

The countess was right. Lydia was given every dirty chore to do. She was made to scoop out the latrines with her bare hands, dig graves and wash down corpses of the women that had died in her hut. It was not long before Lydia became ill. She contracted scarlet fever.

In a way this illness was in fact her saving, for she was moved to the camp hospital for ten days and was able, in this way, to rest and gather back some of the strength she had lost. The hospital was a palace compared to the hut. There were clean white sheets on the beds even though the beds were just as hard as the bunks at Block 32. The hospital was in the care of a woman known as Frau Lehman. She was chosen to look after the old, elderly and the sick. Never has a hospital been in charge of such a matron. She was responsible for sending more women than anyone else to the crematorium. Due to Lydia's age, she made a fairly rapid recovery. Sleep was what she needed more than anything else — and food. Hospital patients were given just a little better nourishment than the rest of the camp and although this was nevertheless still a starvation diet, it seemed like a banquet to be able to eat plates of hot, thin potato soup and mashed lumpy potatoes with one's crust of stale bread.

Not long afterwards Lydia was ill again but this time there was no hospital treatment for her. She had dysentery. And dysentery was a normal disease. Everyone, at some time or another at the camp, had dysentery. Those who suffered from this terrible sickness were made to line up before three tubs and wash each other down. Women who appeared to be half skeleton half human being were sitting in tubs that were filled more with excreta than with water. A nauseating, pitiful sight. Girls of twenty looked nearer sixty and those of sixty died or were sent, half dead, to the crematorium.

Again Lydia's youth and courage saved her. And it was shortly after this illness that she decided that something ought to be done to keep up the morale of the hut. Things were becoming increasingly worse. Women were so hungry they would have turned to cannibalism — as indeed one or two did shortly before they, too, were consumed by the flames of the crematorium.

It was Lydia's job that decided her on doing something about morale. As she was able-bodied and young, she was picked with about six hundred others to go to the nearby Siemens factory. Ravensbrück was fifty miles from Berlin and the massive factory stood between it and the capital. It was at the Siemens works that Lydia slaved from 6 a.m. until 6 p.m. with no more than ten minutes off for lunch. The latter consisted of dry bread and a mug of ersatz coffee. Some of the German workers at the factory took pity on the slaves around them and handed out the odd pieces of chocolate, sausage and cheese and Lydia felt almost happy during the six months she worked there. She never had any idea what it was she helped to make. The section into which she was placed made electric springs — but all Lydia did was press a button at regular intervals.

The button became a part of her life. She dreamed of that button, had nightmares about it. 'You must press this button so, like this,' the German foreman had told her. 'If you do not press it when this light here shows red, you will ruin the whole thing and then you'll be for it I can promise you that. Understood?' For twelve hours each day, Lydia pressed that button, forcing herself to keep awake for if she closed her eyes for only a few seconds, she would miss the red light and the button would not be pressed. That would be tragic. Some of the other girls had already been severely whipped for forgetting a little detail such as not pressing their button or some other mechanical gadget they had to pull or push at intervals.

And so back at the camp, in her hut, where morale was at its lowest ebb and morals were even lower, Lydia discussed her plan with the countess.

'I was thinking, if we were to sing a few songs at night or recite poetry or something like that, it would help pass the time away until the war is over. And the war can surely not last very much longer. What do you feel about it?'

'An excellent idea, my child, excellent,' the countess smiled approval. 'Of course, most of us are too weak to sing songs or recite but, at least, those who are strong enough would help the others get stronger.'

Someone or other had obtained a comb and someone else a piece of thin paper. This formed the only musical instrument in the band, the percussion being performed by the feet and clapping hands. And so, in the evenings, when the women were able to congregate in their hut after 7 p.m., they sang quietly and danced until lights out an hour later. Lydia was the star of the shows. She performed little ballets for the women and never had so appreciative an audience. She hummed the melody while she danced and those who knew the tune would join in. Women forgot their weakness, their lice and their diseases. They forgot the horrors of their forced existence for one brief hour and enjoyed life. They even went as far as to make up little poems of their own to recite and composed simple songs to sing.

Lydia also organized keep-fit classes and lectured to the women on the right and the wrong way to breathe.

'Hey, Lydia,' called a woman of some forty years who looked much older and who was as thin as a stick. 'How can I keep my beautifully slim figure?' This caused a roar of laughter. Lydia had won them over. Morale rose by leaps and bounds.

Until Fräulein Binz stepped in.

For almost two weeks the nightly 'shows' and keep-fit classes had continued without any interruption. The noise coming from the huts in the Block was great enough during the hour before lights out to drown any sing-songs. The chattering of thousands of women was enough to dampen any festivities and Binz never suspected that in one of those huts people were actually dancing and singing, reciting poetry and doing knees-bend-arms-stretch exercises. But on that particular night Binz decided to make one of her tours of inspection. She did this whenever she wanted to make someone taste the sting of her whip and the lash of her tongue. Two girls in Lydia's hut took turns to keep a look-out for Binz. Even Lise took her turn, for despite her relationship with the Block Commandant, she, too, was a prisoner and she, too, wanted to join in any extraordinary activities such as those organized by Lydia Lipski. She had never told Binz of these 'shows'. She knew that any treachery on her part would have resulted in her being torn limb from limb by the inmates of her hut.

That night the look-outs were two Polish girls and Lydia was dancing her choreography of Chopin's Polonaise. It was too good for the girls watching out for guards and Binz, and they joined in the humming of the tune and watched Lydia dance when the door burst open and a furious Binz stood before them.

'What the hell do you think you're doing!' exclaimed Binz after the humming had died down to an embarrassed silence. Lise was the first to speak. 'We were only having a little fun this evening, Fraulein Binz. You see it's the birthday of...'

'I don't give a goddamn whose birthday it is, but whoever it is who's responsible for this outrage will wish she'd never been born,' Binz interrupted shouting furiously, her blonde hair almost standing on end. 'You!' (pointing her whip at Lydia) 'I told you that the next time I had any trouble from you I'd kill you. And by Christ that's just about what I'm going to do....' And she advanced on Lydia who stood her ground defiantly. Binz slapped her across the face with the handle of her whip until Lydia lost consciousness. This is it, thought Lydia. This is my moment. And she silently prayed to God and asked Him to receive her soul and forgive her sins. But she received the beating without so much as a whimper. Again, as she lay on the floor, Binz kicked her in the hip and spat upon her. Then she turned upon the others who looked on in horror and in silence.

'You are here to work not play,' screamed Binz looking about her. 'And just as a special birthday treat, I'm putting this hut on half rations for a week. I shall also place a permanent guard outside here for the duration of that week and if I get so much as a whisper out of any of you, there'll be no rations at all. Understood?' And she swept out.

Half rations! Whole rations meant a tiny piece of bread in the morning, watery soup for lunch and more watery soup in the evening, except for those who lunched at the factory when the cup of ersatz coffee was provided by the Siemens canteen. After that interrupted party, no bread at all was distributed and the soup consisted of just a few spoonfuls.

However, Lydia was not to be beaten so easily. If they could no longer sing or dance, then she was determined to find some other method of keeping morale high. When a person suffers every degradation imaginable, when the chimney of the crematorium continues to belch smoke from its bowels, when skin clings half-heartedly to bone, when whiplashes are generous and food low, when death is for ever peeping round the corner beckoning young and old, then one either surrenders to one's fate, gives in completely and allows the body to wither and die or one rises above the dangers, defies death, spits in his eye and enters the realms of heroism. Lydia took the latter course. She felt that she had nothing to lose except her life and, since it was almost certain that she was meant to die in this Bridge of Graves, she constantly thought of ways and means to make death easier. She was determined to die bravely, a credit to her family and to her honour. The Countess de Ganay had been her greatest influence. Lydia had taken her advice and kept clean. Now she was trying to persuade the others to do the same.

As soon as she found herself capable of speaking, she organized relays of women to go to the wash basins, explaining that if they were to wash themselves thoroughly every morning, no matter what the weather, they would not be as open to disease as they were at present. So the hut's reveille was brought forward by an hour and the relays began. Women washed themselves quickly but well and the constant squabbling ceased. They continued with their keep-fit exercises individually, slowly standing on their toes and stretching up their arms while breathing in deeply and coming down on their heels, slowly dropping their arms as they breathed out. Each would perform this ritual twenty times and, though their nostrils were filled with the stench of death, they gradually began to feel more human. Even the old went through the routine, pathetically, achingly stretching their bones up towards the sky. They did not want to be left out of this one last chance to live.

And there was yet another escapist programme that Lydia instigated. 'If the body needs cleanliness in order to keep alive, then so does the soul,' she told her motley companions in the hut. Most of the inmates were Catholics, so Mass was held in the hut every Sunday. There was no priest. 'We must each be our own priest,' said Lydia. 'God will understand — and He will hear our prayers.' And so, on Sundays almost everyone would kneel down and recite the mass quietly as best as they could remember it.

Even the non-Catholics that were present from Germany and Holland knelt down and recited their own prayers. Each Sunday one of the women would prepare a sermon in her own language. Even if the others could not understand, most were by now able to make sense of some of the other's languages and feel the meaning of the words. Lydia spoke the first sermon and the Countess de Ganay held it on the second Sunday. Hers was simple and straight forward.

'My friends,' she began. 'I am an old woman now. I have seen many things in my days on this earth and I realize that class and creed do not enter a prison, particularly a prison such as this one. Here we are all equals. We are suffering the same pain, the same disease, the same anguish. Some of us may have been brought up with riches and love and have never wanted for anything. Others may have been brought up in poverty and need. Here we are all poor. Here we are all in need of affection. Some of us have been brought up in different countries from others, speaking different languages. Here we stand on the same ground, under the same roof and we speak the same words even if they sometimes sound different. We call out our pain in the same way, make felt our hunger in the same way, we are sick in the same way.

'We have been united here because many of us had either openly fought the German Nazis, or displeased them in some way.

'Many of our sisters lie dead, burned or starved or beaten. They have gone out to meet their Maker just as all of us here will one day do. We may all die here today or tomorrow or we may live to tell the tales of horror and of man's inhumanity to man when the war is over and we return to our homes. But even if we survive death here, we cannot survive it. One day we must all bid this life farewell, leave this cruel earth and stand in judgment before the King of Kings. What sort of judgment will He pass upon you and me? My dear friends, you may rejoice. God is here just as He was here on earth two thousand years ago. He is witnessing your misery just as He is witnessing the cruelty of those who have imprisoned us. His judgment upon us will be, I am sure, a fair one, for He will say that we have suffered all that any of us can be expected to suffer. The life He will offer us hereafter will be one of peace and believe me, I know, for I can almost smell the flowers of Paradise at this moment. I have not much longer to live, my dear friends, and I rejoice, for I know that I may look forward to my rest up there with Him.

'And how will he judge those who have broken every one of His commandments? How will he judge those who have murdered and burned and raped? How will He judge those who have robbed, who have trodden upon their neighbours and their neighbours' wives, their land and cattle?

'Why, my friends, he will judge them fairly too. They who have danced around the golden calf will find that the gold has melted and become lead and that the lead has entwined itself around their necks. There will be no great tidal waves to come and drown them, no fire sent from heaven to burn them up. There will only be conscience — their conscience and the conscience of

[143]

their children and their children's children. And their deeds will be written down in history and for the rest of eternity the world will point at them and say; "we pity you for we know that you fully know what you have done".

'I know that it is difficult to turn and cull from the Holy Book the incidents of turning the other cheek. We have turned both cheeks and we have turned them again and again and our cheeks bleed from the beatings, our hearts ache with the sorrow of those who have been tortured in our presence and away from us, and our bodies cry out for peace and rest.

'I know, too, that it must be even more difficult for us to quote Our Lord and say: "Forgive them Father — for they know not what they do" because firstly they know exactly what they do and secondly because we cannot compare ourselves, however lowly, with Christ the Saviour. He died in order to save the world. We die merely in order to accuse it.

'And so, my friends, we are left with one solution. That solution lies deep in our hearts and it is prayer. God will not expect you to pray for forgiveness for those who are beating you, for those who trespass against us, for we have no forgiveness left ourselves and cannot expect others to hand it out on our behalf. He will not expect you to pray for your daily bread, for He can see the daily bread that is being distributed. Instead remember only the other lines of the Lord's Prayer: "Thy Kingdom come on earth as it is in Heaven and deliver us from evil." Then shall His name be hallowed. Then, my friends, shall we have peace — everlasting. In the name of the Father and the Son and the Holy Ghost, Amen.'

Two weeks later the Countess de Ganay was dead. She died of starvation.

CHAPTER THIRTEEN:

FRIENDSHIPS AND TEMPTATIONS

Whenever the camp authorities could find nothing for the inmates to do, then the order would go out for individual Block Commanders to parade their prisoners around the block. No matter what the weather, no matter what the condition of the individual prisoners, all were made to come out and march round and round the block enclosure in single file and in their bare feet. Feet became red and swollen; they would bleed and ache and become infested with dirt. In some cases gangrene set in and many women had to have their feet, and sometimes their legs amputated. This was generally done without any proper anaesthetic and the majority who endured the operation died shortly afterwards. Nor was there any opportunity to rest during these meaningless marches. As soon as one person fell or slowed down, guards dragged them to their feet and whipped them on.

It is little wonder that so many of the women, bereft of love and living continually in pain and fear, should turn to one another for affection. Lesbianism was not so much a vice as a necessity. Often during the night there could be heard the little words of endearment normally only spoken between lovers. They craved each other's spare warmth and few had any warmth to spare during the cold winter months. Hungry lips sought hungry lips. Emaciated bodies entwined and minds made belief that this was a man holding them, that these lips were the lips of a man. Ersatz love they called it even as they embraced and cold sweat trickled between their milkless breasts and the wooden bunks creaked with the ecstasy.

Two of the girls in Lydia's hut became constant lovers and remained such until well after the war had ended. One was twenty-two. The other twenty-five. It was the latter who, after the war, changed her sex completely. And the two were married in the mid fifties.

Lydia only entered into the realms of lesbianism for a brief period—and then more out of pity than for the effects of it. In the hut was a young girl called Maria Czelenski. This seventeen-year-old Czech girl was quite ugly and her face and body was covered in pimples. No one ever attempted to befriend her — except Lydia, for she could see that Maria was more lonely, more frightened and more silent than any of the others. One evening Lydia approached her. The French girl had 'inherited' the top bunk of the late Countess de Ganay and had it to herself for the present.

'Hello, Maria. You're always so very quiet and look so very sad. Would you like to tell me about it?'

Maria looked surprised. No one had ever spoken kindly to her since she had come to Ravensbrück. And here was Lydia talking to her as though they had been close friends for years and years — and Lydia was the most respected of all the girls in the hut even if she was not the hut leader.

'Thank you for asking, but I — I'd rather not talk about it.' Oh, but really she wanted so much to do so — particularly to Lydia. Why had she said such a silly thing? Not talk about it! Of course she wanted to.

'All right,' said Lydia. 'But remember, if ever you should change your mind, I shall always be willing to listen. All right?'

'Yes, thank you. Thank you so very much,' the girl answered, and cast her eyes at the floor. Then, as Lydia was about to turn and walk away, she clutched at her arm. 'Wait. Please wait. I — I'm sorry if I appeared rude just now. Of course I'd like to talk to you, dearest Lydia. You see, I don't know what has become of my parents or my brothers and sisters.'

'How many brothers and sisters have you, Maria?'

'Well, there were nine of us. Four girls and five boys. But you see I was sent away from home to an uncle in Prague who said he'd look after me. But he didn't and so I ran away and hid and then joined the Underground.'

'I see. And then you were caught and ended up here and now you don't know where your parents are, is that it? Well, I'm sure they are quite safe and your brothers and sisters are probably more worried about you than you are about them. Why not say a prayer for them all instead of being always so sad, eh?'

'Oh I do, I do. I pray every night and every morning when I wake up and in my mind I burn thousands of candles for them — but you see I heard such dreadful stories since I came here and I don't know what to believe. I think, you see, that they may all be dead.'

'Why, what a silly thing to say,' said Lydia as though speaking to a little child and forgetting that she herself was little more than Maria's age. 'I'm sure there is nothing at all to worry about and that they are still at home exactly where you last saw them. Where is your home by the way?'

'I come from Lidice.'

Lydia stiffened and a cold shiver ran along her spine. She quickly composed herself and hoped Maria had not noticed her shock. 'Lidice? I'm sorry, I don't think I've ever heard of that place before. I'm Polish, you see, by birth.'

'Oh, it's only a small town. Everyone knew everyone else, you know. Only — only — some of the new arrivals here from Czechoslovakia say the Germans burned the whole place to the ground and — and killed everyone.'

Maria burst into a flood of tears — the first she had openly shed since her arrival one year earlier. Lydia took Maria's head in both her hands and pressed it against her breasts. 'Now, now, Maria, you're a big girl now. You mustn't cry. And you mustn't believe that story you heard because it simply is not true. I've not heard it and if there is any story going around I am usually one of the first to be told. You know that all the new arrivals come to me and give me the latest from the outside world.'

Maria stopped sobbing and looked up at Lydia. 'Honest? D'you mean you've not been told those things about the burning and the gas chambers — mobile ones in the street — and all that? D'you think it's a lie?' her eyes pleaded confirmation.

'Of course it's a lie. Some of these people from outside exaggerate a lot of things. They just want us to believe they've seen more terrible things than we have. But that story is certainly not true because I've not even heard of Li — what was it? Lidice. There now, feel better?'

'Oh yes, thank you, Lydia. You don't know how much better you've made me feel.' And for the first time since Lydia had seen Maria, she smiled. And Lydia returned the smile. But in her heart she wept, for she had heard of the massacre of Lidice. She knew the story was true.

'Would you like to come and sleep with me tonight, Maria?' She did not know why she asked the question. But she felt sorry for the child.

Maria looked long at Lydia searching her face for a reason. 'No one has ever asked me that before. I — I know I'm so ugly and.'

'No, no, you must not think that. You're not at all ugly. You're very pretty, really you are! And if people have not asked you — well, it's only because — because you've been so quiet and kept away from everyone. Perhaps they thought it was you who did not like them. Has that never occurred to you, Maria?'

And so it was that Lydia took Maria to her bunk and lavished kisses upon her. It was an act of compassion, of mercy. It was the love this little girl could never again receive from her own mother. And Lydia thought of her brother and mother who had gone to Poland and wondered if the same sort of fate had overcome them. And she, too, cried and prayed.

Lydia continued to press her little button at the factory and the machine eventually turned out electric springs. During the first few months at the camp she had been made to work in the same way as most of the prisoners — cleaning out the latrines, walking barefooted some three miles dragging a cart, filling it with coal from a heap and dragging it back again, filling wheel-barrows with sand and tipping it out a mile or so further away. It was in this way that the guards saw that this girl was fairly strong.

The guards were right. Lydia was certainly strong. Despite the starvation diet and despite her weight which had dropped to a mere six stones, her decision to keep herself constantly clean and her morale high, also helped her body to endure more physical strain than it might otherwise have accepted. It was her apparent strength that brought her the job at the Siemens factory. But the strain of pressing a button had its effects at night when, trying to sleep in the snake-pit of a hut, she found difficulty in breathing. At least, during her work at the camp she had been in the open, semi-fresh air. Now she was cooped up inside a building from early morning until night and saw the sky only through a distant window. At night all she was able to breathe in was the stench of other women's sweaty bodies, the vomit of the sick, the excreta of those suffering from dysentery. If only she could breathe some fresh air at night, thought Lydia, how much easier it would be to sleep well.

Her prayer seemed to be answered. For, one day at the factory, she spotted a small saw lying underneath her machine. How it had found its way there she did not know — and didn't care. She watched that saw all day long. It hypnotized her. If only she could smuggle it out of the factory and into the camp before someone came to collect it. No one came. No one else seemed to have seen it. In the evening, as the whistle blew and the huge mechanism that rattled on throughout the day, drowning all thoughts, ground wearily to a halt, she picked it up and secreted it under her dress.

No one searched her, either on her way out of the factory or on her way into the camp — searches were frequently held on every third, fourth or fifth person leaving the factory. She had managed to smuggle into her hut a saw, a little insignificant saw — the most precious article she had ever possessed. With that saw, in the dead of night, she began cutting herself a hole above her head, a small hole alongside the roof of the hut. After a few nights she had managed to cut out a small square some two inches by one inch — and the air and sky suddenly belonged to her. She breathed in the precious oxygen and fell peacefully asleep.

The following Sunday, after Mass, when prisoners were allowed an hour's rest, Lydia lay on her bunk looking up through her little private window and counted the clouds moving overhead. There were not many clouds, for it was summer, a stifling hot, summer's day, but to Lydia those clouds presented hope and freedom. She saw faces in those clouds, faces that smiled down at her, that seemed to say 'it won't be long now and you'll be able to drift along like us in peace'. The blue sky and those little whispy faces reminded her of Nice and the beach and the blue Mediterranean and her childhood. Lydia basked in her dreams. Concentration camp or no, she thought, they cannot take away my dreams. And she smiled up at the clouds and they seemed to smile back down at her.

'What the hell have you done, you *Schweinfranzösin*?' The harsh spitting voice of Fräulein Binz shook Lydia from her reverie and she sat up with a start. Now she would be really for it, she thought. Binz caught hold of Lydia by the hair and dragged her down to the ground with a bump. 'Always it's you! Always you! You're no good for anything! How the hell have you managed to make that hole up there? Eh? Answer me! How did you do it? With your teeth? With your nails? By Christ, if you don't answer me, I'll beat the living daylight out of you.' And Binz whipped Lydia murderously, lashing her body until the blood turned her grey uniform to red. Then, as Lydia lay senseless on the ground, Binz called a guard. 'As soon as she comes round, you will take her before the Camp Commandant, understand? This little pig is going to pay for this wanton damage. She'll pay for it very dearly. All right, the rest of you, what the hell are you all gawping for? Get on with your work. You've rested quite enough. I'm sick to death of the lot of you. *Was für eine Schweinerei! Ein Schweinestall habt ihr euch hier gemacht. Das stinkt ja dauernd nur von Scheisse!* God send the day when you're all burned and gone. You're not worth keeping alive — any of you!' And she stamped out using her whip liberally upon anyone who stood too close to her path.

Hubert Schwatz could not believe his ears. *'Was hat sie getan? Ein Loch? Ein Loch ins Dach? Na, was hör' ich den da? Ein richtiges Loch?'* He could not believe that anyone would actually dare create a hole in a roof. This, surely, was the height of vandalism! Such a thing was no doubt a personal insult to the Fuehrer who had been good enough to build these excellent huts for these scum of women who did not even know how to live properly! Lydia stood weakly before him, hardly able to control her legs which felt as though they were about to fall off, away from the rest of her sore and bleeding body. Her mouth was dry and she swallowed her own blood gratefully for it wet her parched throat.

'So.... So....' Schwatz was pacing up and down thinking. He was obviously trying to decide whether to have the girl thrown to the ovens, or whether she might prove more useful elsewhere. 'So... so... ein Loch... so' and he continued to pace the floor with short, rapid strides, his podgy hands clasped behind his back and his face screwed up in an agony of thought. It must be very difficult to decide on the cruelest way to execute a person. Hanging? thought Schwatz. No too good, too quick. Burning alive? That's better but... He stopped and stepped back behind his desk. His face had unscrewed itself and now took on the cruel mask of Schwatz the Judge.

'I shall not permit such hooliganism in this camp. You have committed a very grave crime and the punishment must, therefore, also be a grave one. However, because of your youth and because I have had good reports about you from the *Werke* (the Siemens Works) I have decided not to sentence you to death and I trust you realize how generous I have been with you this time. No, instead I sentence you to an indefinite period, not to be shorter than one month, in the *Strafblock*. Take her away.' The trial was over and the Judge resumed his seat. He forgot all about the incident at once and continued to write his letters.

'My dearest Röschen,' began one such document. 'The sun is shining and all around me birds are singing such pretty songs. How I wish we were together at this moment, able to share the beauties of nature....'

Whoever his Rose was — and she was certainly not his wife — she seemed to mean more to him than the stench of burning bodies. But then, Herr Kommandant Hubert Schwatz had no conscience. Once this war was over, he would be able to tell the Nuremberg judges in all sincerity that 'I was only carrying out orders.'

His latest order had been to send a young French girl to the *Strafblock*. This was the punishment block of Ravensbrück — as though the rest of the camp was not already sufficient punishment. Most women would have rather died than enter it. Lydia had heard about it and now recalled that she had never again seen those who had been confined there.

What she did not know was that at the *Strafblock* men and women who called themselves doctors carried out experiments on women prisoners. She did not know that the prisoners who entered there were known as the camp's *Kanninchen* (rabbits), for they were the rabbits — or guinea pigs — to come under the 'doctors' and their knives.*

---

*Prisoners were chosen for experiments from the *Nacht und Nebel* block and not only from the *Strafblock*. But the 'doctors' were more liberal in picking their victims from the punishment block.

[150]

Each prisoner who entered the block was made to add a black circle to the triangle and number already on the uniform. Guards handed out those black circles as though they were medals. It was true that anyone who survived the tortures there deserved a medal. Lydia sewed on her black circle carefully, not knowing what the future held. She certainly did not know that she was the very first French woman to enter that black hole.

No one worked in the *Strafblock*. The prisoners were too weak to work. They were too weak because they were put into solitary confinement in a series of holes. They saw no light. They breathed no air. They were made to spend the first four days without food of any description. And then if they were still alive, they were put through a series of endurance tests. Their bodies were immersed in ice cold water until they almost drowned. They were then revived and immersed in baths of hot water until they wished they could drown. But again they would be revived.

If any of these 'patients' could not endure the tests and, indeed, died — well, it did not matter. They were thrown on marble slabs and carefully dissected. The doctors were 'doing their duty'. They were performing experiments 'in the name of science and for the good of the Fatherland'.

And it was to this hell's pit that Lydia de Korczac Lipski, then aged nineteen, was thrown.

CHAPTER FOURTEEN:

OF DOCTORS AND RABBITS

T he Herr Doktor Gustav Fischer ordered Lydia to strip and regarded her frail body with contempt. She won't last long he thought, but she seemed cleaner than a lot of the others he had been sent. Fischer was fat and in his early forties. His blond, Aryan hair was combed straight back from his thick receding forehead. An ugly scar, won with honour at a University of Göttingen Corporation *Mensur* (duel) during his salad days as a medical student, almost gleamed along the whole of his left cheek. Fischer enjoyed his work. He had graduated from Göttingen with Honours and from the concentration camp of Auschwitz with the Iron Cross First Class. He had seen the living squirm under his knife and die. It did not bother Dr. Fischer. His experiments were all carried out in the name of the Fatherland and of science. He recalled that during his undergraduate days, when he was poor and struggling to obtain his degree, several Jewish students passed exams easily, qualified as members of a noble profession without so much as a single headache. He had failed his finals twice. The Jews had passed, he remembered, mostly at their first attempt. Those Jews. They never seemed to join in the drinking parties; they never seemed to be interested in women; never fought duels; abnormal cowards, those Jews.

But he had had his revenge on the Jews at Auschwitz. There they were no longer the proud, select, chosen people. There they were meek and crawling. He had enjoyed seeing camp barbers shaving them of their orthodox beards and their long black hair and the dentists tugging out their gold teeth. Oh, that was fun. Jews without their hair, bald Jews with their accentuated long noses and toothless mouths amused him. They looked just like those cartoons he had laughed at in the *Stürmer*. Fischer blessed the name of Adolf Hitler who had realized that the Jews were a menace to Germany and the great Aryan race and had decided to exterminate them from the face of the earth. But Fischer, the experienced, highly esteemed doctor, had been transferred to Ravensbrück to teach others his methods, perform his experiments on women. And these women were not even Jews. Some were actually Germans. At first Dr. Fischer could not understand that there could be other people whom Hitler wanted exterminated. But it did not take him long to fall in with the ideals of the Fatherland. He would not flinch from his duties. Never! The Jews were not the only scum in the world. After all, the Polacks were — well, almost Jews. Many looked Jewish. As for the Italians and the French — there was hardly any difference. Every time he inserted his knife into a Polish breast, he imagined it was, in fact, a Jew going to meet his Maker. Fischer had no quarrels with his conscience. He was clean; a good doctor.

His stethoscope was now prodding and skipping over Lydia's body. He listened to her heart. It was beating fast. She was afraid. Good, thought Fischer. It is good when prisoners are afraid. Here was another damn Polack. No, he thought, she would not last long. He examined her mouth and throat, her ears and proceeded to give her a thorough gynaecological exam. He only carried out such exams on the younger prisoners. The old ones were of no interest to him, made him feel nauseated even. But the young ones — especially the pretty ones — that was different and he could take his time. Lydia felt sick. He was hurting her and she bit her lips to stave off one pain with another. Fischer made notes on a chart by his side. *'Abtreten'* he finally ordered. The consultation was ended and Lydia was taken to her cell.

Cell! The term conjures up a picture of near luxury to those familiar with modern prisons. In the *Strafblock* there was no luxury. Lydia's cell was a hole without any window, without air, without bed or bedding, without any sanitary convenience. There was only the stench of those who had been there before her and her cell-mates consisted of fleas, lice and bugs that crawled in disorganized armies over her body day and night, drinking her blood and growing fat while she grew thinner. Could this, then, be hell? Lydia thought she had been to hell already — a thousand hells. But none had come down to these standards. How much had one to suffer before being cleansed of one's sins? Lydia gave up trying to think of the answer.

Even her stomach had given up all hopes of being fed. It had stopped rumbling its request and surrendered to feeding its last remaining juices to the parasitic bugs. Lydia's dreams were invaded by outsize steaks and fried potatoes, by trees whose branches were weighed down with a profusion of oranges and bananas and apples and blocks of chocolate all growing together waiting for her to pick. But, when she tried to clutch at them, she found she could not reach high enough. When she attempted to climb the trees of her dreams, the trunk was slippery and she fell down on hard mountains of burned meat. She awoke to the smell of her own flesh, prostrate upon a hard and dirty stone floor. The things were still creeping over her, sucking her dry.

During her first week at the *Strafblock* she was examined daily by doctors. Sometimes it was Dr. Fischer. On other days it was his chief assistant, Dr. Rudolf Treiter, a solidly built little man whose greatest pleasure was to ill-treat and eventually strangle his own patients. All in the name of science. He was able to note down just how long it took between the hand's pressure upon the throat and the last terrible breath. Treiter, it was, who attempted various methods of artificial respiration and heart massage to revive the corpse. In two or three cases he was successful and brought the patient 'back to life' for a few minutes. But he merely strangled them again and made his notes.

Then there was Dr. Hans Gerhart who, before the war, had been the senior resident at the Hohenlichen sanatorium. He had been well liked there. A marvellous doctor, the patients had said, such a wonderful bedside manner. There was nothing bedsideish about Dr. Gerhart at Ravensbrück. Together with the official camp doctor — Dr. Schidlowski — he performed the most gruesome experiments upon a group of Polish women. Two hundred of them had been sent from Lublin and Warsaw. They were known as 'The Seven Thousand' because their prisoner numbers came in the 7,000 range.

Schidlowski and Gerhart performed their experiments with great precision. The patient would be laid out on the operating table, given a mild anesthetic to keep her quiet, and the operation would begin. Whole bones and muscles were removed from the patients' legs as was the skin. These were then sent to German military hospitals where they were grafted to the legs of wounded German soldiers. Most of the women died after these experiments. What remained of their bodies was burned in the camp crematorium. Some survived. They were never able to walk again. Their mutilated, deformed legs served as a reminder of the most savage, most bestial period of Man's history. Many of the survivors had their legs amputated after the war, thus curtailing their memories.

Some of the stronger women, who managed to survive one such operation, were made to undergo another. Only two or three came out alive of their second ordeal. One young girl, a friend of Lydia's, was one of those very few. Leonka Bien underwent five such operations within four weeks. After the fifth her body was also sent to the crematorium. Leonka Bien was just eighteen years old.

A woman named Baika who also managed to live on after the experiments, was liberated from the camp after the war and taken to a British military hospital. There she had her leg cut open once again. She had complained of dreadful pains in her left leg. When British surgeons opened up the leg, they found a bobbin of thread and a needle inside. The Herren Doktoren Gerhart and Schidlowski had not even tried to be careful.

Other experiments consisted of removing skin from the scalp, transposing skin from one prisoner to another to see how long it would take for it to graft — or for the prisoner to die. Brain operations were also favourite pastimes with the doctors. The scalp would be slit open and certain brain nerves severed. The patient would be stitched up again and the result observed. What part of the brain governed what part of the human system? It was this question the doctors wanted to have answered.

It did not horrify the doctors to see the results of their tortures. They showed genuine interest in how their patients, who were totally or partially paralysed, turned into gibbering idiots and blinded or made speechless. The only ones in whom they lost all medical interest were the dead. Some of these were dissected in order to divulge where the scalpel had gone wrong. But most of them were sent directly to the crematorium. Their bodies would only make the place stench more than it already did if they were not immediately burned. It was all in the name of science, starry-eyed science, in a Satanic school.

Lydia grew frail and weak. She had been in the *Strafblock* four weeks and was even being fed now. Thin potato soup and a crust of bread was the staple diet of the prisoners there — just enough to keep them from dying and sufficiently healthy to be carved up by the doctors. By now, the beautiful girl whose crime it had been to help her father in the fight to save France from corruption and the jackboot, was no more than a bundle of skin and bones. Her body was covered in sores showing exactly where the bugs had bitten her. Her mouth was dry and her teeth hung loosely from constantly bleeding gums. The doctors still continued to examine her and make notes. They wanted to see just how much a human being could endure before shaking hands with death.

One day, during her fifth week in hell, she was brought before Gerhart. He was dressed in white overalls, the doctor's uniform, and held a hypodermic needle in his hands.

'Come and lie down over here and pull down your dress,' he said quite calmly as though Lydia was one of his Hohenlichen sanatorium patients come to his spotless surgery. There, the inmates would have willingly pulled down their dresses for him, gone without a murmur to his operating table. There, he had been trusted, liked, even loved by some of the middle-aged women. For Gerhart was, himself, not old — in his late thirties — and could have been described as handsome were it not for the bitter downward curl of his mouth that stood constantly at twenty-past-eight.

Lydia, however, was not in love with him. She was not one of his sanatorium fans. She did not trust him. She knew her time had come for an operation. And Lydia screamed.

'Please shoot me,' she shouted. 'Why, in God's name don't you just shoot me here on the spot? Wouldn't that be just as good as one of your devilish operations? You swine, you monster! D'you call yourself a doctor? D'you dare to go on living and call yourself a doctor? Does the oath you took mean nothing to you? Go on, Doctor, shoot me! I'd rather be dead than go on through this living death…'

Gerhart stood stunned for a moment. How dare this snip of a girl insult him in this manner! The two nurses who were in attendance looked on shocked. No one had ever spoken to the Herr Doktor Gerhart in this fashion. Oh, yes, they had all screamed, the fools. But their screams had been pleading. They had screamed for fear, had promised the doctor everything, had begged him on their bended knees to let them be. But this girl! She had actually cursed, insulted the man, questioned his ability as a man of medicine.

Gerhart put down his needle and advanced on Lydia. His face had regained its cruel composure. He slapped her face very hard several times until she collapsed. As she lay on the ground, he kicked her brutally in the ribs and spat into her face.

'Now stand her up,' he ordered the nurses who came and picked Lydia up forcing her to stand straight and to attention. Gerhart returned to his needle and his calm voice as though nothing had transpired. 'I am not going to operate on you,' he said, speaking quietly. 'You are not worth operating and your skin is far too vile to be given to our gallant fighting men. No, I am not going to operate. Just a little injection that's all. A little injection.' He had regained his bedside manner. 'It won't even hurt. You won't feel a thing, I promise you.'

The nurses — one of whom was a fat creature called Erika who had herself strangled prisoners to death — clasped Lydia's struggling body in a grip of iron, while Dr. Gerhart advanced, needle in hand. The injection was given in her right arm. It did not last long and Lydia, already so full of pain, did not even feel the prick.

[156]

Gerhart replaced the hypodermic onto his side table next to the other instruments of torture and turned to Lydia. She was still being held by the two women who called themselves nurses. Her face was ashen grey and her tears had dried on her cheeks. What had he done to her, she wondered. At any moment she expected herself to go limp, fall into a deep narcosis and awake some hours later without her limbs. But instead she heard the doctor say:

'There, I told you it would not hurt. You may go away now. The injection I have given you is of a very special nature. You will feel absolutely no reactions to it — not for about twenty-five years, if my calculations are right, and I am certain that they are quite correct. You should feel honoured. You are the very first I have tried this experiment on. In twenty-five years you will feel the reactions. Then we shall see what we shall see. So. *Abtreten!*' Gerhart turned away to wash his hands.

And Lydia was dragged back to her hole and the fleas, the lice and the bugs.

The experiment was made in November, 1944. The twenty-five-year period would be up in November, 1969. Lydia never had the slightest idea what reactions, if any, she might expect. But the nightmare remained constantly with her. Doctors examined her after the war, but found nothing to indicate what serum had been injected. It remained a mystery.

One might well ask oneself why such a long-term experiment was carried out on someone who had been placed into the *Nacht und Nebel* Block 32 — the section whose prisoners were fated to die, to be transported to the 'shower baths'. The answer lies logically in the philosophy of Nazi Germany. Hitler had made his plans for a thousand-year Reich. His dreams of a Germany that would dominate the whole world spread over a period of one hundred decades in the minutest detail. His ideal was that Germany should become the greatest nation of all, that it should wield more power than the Romans ever did. Twenty-five years was, in the minds of those who had been chosen to help attain this power for the Third Reich, therefore, a mere breath. Young doctors were especially aware of the miracles they might be able to achieve in the name of the Führer. They dreamed of riches and of academic fame in the same way as doctors do today. Not all were concerned with killing their victims. Butchery on the operating table was a pleasant enough pastime. But some experiments — such as Lydia's — were carried out seriously and with an eye on great achievements of the future.

Among the inmates of Ravensbrück were many Hungarian and Polish gypsies. These were immediately herded into the *Strafblock* to become 'rabbits.' All were sterilized. They included children aged between twelve and fourteen. The prettier ones were sent to the camp brothel where they were raped (or gave themselves willingly) nightly by the camp staff. Children were considered a delicacy and were forced to perform the vilest sexual perversions before being set upon by the men who worked at the camp as guards or in the administrative buildings or in the extermination quarters. The victims who became pregnant were sent to the 'doctors'. In the Strafblock they were allowed to grow fat. Many, because of starvation diets and ill treatment, had miscarriages within the first five or six months of pregnancy. Others, however, were well treated and allowed to live until the labour period was almost due. Then the doctors would perform the abortion. It was rare that the mother survived the operation. Those who did and who did not die before Ravensbrück was liberated spent the rest of their lives in mental homes.

The Nazi regime thought it could take its time over its executions and tortures. How wrong the Nazis were was proved by the steady advances made by the Allies. The invasion of France on D-Day and the gradual liberation of countries under German occupation came as a shock to those who had staunchly believed in Hitler's one thousand-year Reich. History and fate had turned against them.

In January, 1945, Lydia was released from the *Strafblock* half dead, weighing only four stones, and returned to Block 32. There many of the faces had changed. New inmates had arrived to fill the places of those who had died. They now occupied themselves with Lydia, breathing life into her, giving her their meagre rations, washing her wounds and telling her to hold out. 'It cannot last much longer,' they told her. 'The war is almost over. The Germans are being defeated all along the line. The Allies will soon be here and we shall be free, Lydia. Hold out just a little longer. You'll see. Everything will be all right.'

And so Lydia, then twenty, held out and on to the straw of life that was being offered. She looked at the new faces around her and prayed that what they were telling her was true.

Jews were now arriving at the camp. Women and children that looked more like corpses than living human beings were brought in their thousands. They told the inmates of Ravensbrück of the horrors of other camps — camps such as Auschwitz and Belsen. This camp looked luxurious compared with the ones they had come from, they said. Children who had been torn away from their mothers, were later forced to bury their parents' bodies in pits filled with corpses, or were made to roll gas cylinders to the 'showers' where their parents queued up for execution.

Never in the history of the world have so many horrors been recounted by so many in so brief a time. Stories of the starving who turned to cannibalism, eating the dead and the dying because, dear God, there was nothing else left to do.

Stories were told of the snarling, vicious fights between brother and brother over the luxury of a raw, stolen potato....

Stories of those Jews who were too orthodox to touch the little food that was thrown to them because it was *treife* (unclean — not *kasher*) and who died of voluntary starvation — without so much as a murmur. Only a whispered prayer left their lips before their last breath of life: *'Shemah Yisroehl, Adohnei Ehluhehnu, Adohnei Aychott'* (Hear, oh Israel, the Lord is God, the Lord is One).

And there were the stories of those who had been professors, doctors, lawyers, rabbis, being made to eat their own excreta, being made to kiss the Nazi swastika....

Stories of how gold teeth were extracted and melted down to make idols of a horror régime; bodies being skinned and the skin being made into lampshades and canvases for Nazi artists; hair shaved off to produce paint-brushes and rugs; bones and fat being used for the manufacture of soap.

And, incredible though these stories seemed, the real horror was that they were true.

All these tales Lydia heard, stunned, unable to believe that there could be so much cruelty, so much inhumanity to man. The inmates of Ravensbrück listened and looked. And what they heard and saw made their hearts turn cold. So this is what had happened to the Jews! These were the people who had been carried away in the middle of the night from home and business into an inferno of torture. These, then, were God's chosen people, these skeletons with the pathetically shaven skulls, with hollows for eyes. These were the people who had been chosen by God to run, to escape from every torture since the Pharaohs of Ancient Egypt, who had been promised a Land to call home and who had been searching for it ever since Moses brought them out of the Land of Egypt, over the Red Sea and to the River Jordan.

And the crematorium chimney at Ravensbrück belched black smoke throughout the day and night. And the smoke curled up towards Heaven in a mighty question mark.

[159]

CHAPTER FIFTEEN:
THE FIRES OF LIBERTY

If it was the weather or the flames from the crematorium that made February, 1945, seem milder than usual, was no longer clear in Lydia's mind. But she recalled how one day in February, forty women prisoners from Lydia's block were ordered to Binz's office. There they were handed some reasonable clothing (after what they had been accustomed to, anything in the way of clothing seemed reasonable) and a few slices of bread each.

'You are to go on a journey,' Binz told them. The women were overjoyed. Even inside the camp, news had leaked from the far-off world beyond the barbed wire, that the Allies were advancing rapidly and that the war would soon be over. They would be free. With this gesture coming from the normally cruel Fräulein Binz, the women were convinced they were being officially or unofficially allowed to escape.

They were wrong.

The forty women walked away singing — and marched happily towards the crematorium. The chimney spat flames. The 'clean-up' had begun. Binz called another batch of women to her office. Lydia was among them.

'You are to be moved to another camp. I don't know why you've been chosen. You're so much scum, I can't see why you are to be made more comfortable than the others.' Binz was really enjoying herself. 'You will be given clothes and food before setting off on your journey. Count yourselves lucky'

Before the women were called to Binz, they had drawn up a plan of action. They knew that their comrades had been murdered. They were determined not to fall for the same trick. Lydia was still too weak to act as spokesperson for the rest, so a young girl by the name of Jadzia Kaminska was chosen. Whatever was offered or ordered was to be politely but firmly refused.

'So what can they do to us for refusing?' Lydia had argued quietly. 'Kill us? Yes, they can kill us. But if we accept, they also kill us. Let us at least show them that we are not such an easy kill.'

Kaminska took one step forward from the rest of the group. She was visibly trembling but determined to go through with it. 'Fräulein Binz, please,' she said. Binz was surprised. Prisoners never spoke unless spoken to. Who was this child and what did she want? 'Well, what is it?' snapped Binz, feet apart, her hands clasped firmly behind her back.

'On behalf of this group here,' stammered Kaminska, not even daring to look Binz in the eye for fear of forgetting her little speech, meticulously prepared, 'I should like to thank you for your very kind offer....'

Fräulein Binz relaxed slightly. Ye Gods, she thought, a vote of thanks. But she was soon to stiffen up again.

'...but — but we should with respect ask permission to refuse it.'

'Refuse? What the hell do you mean — refuse it?' Binz could hardly credit her ears. 'Have you all gone quite mad?'

'If you wish me to explain, Fräulein Binz,' Jadzia Kaminska proceeded quietly.

'Yes, you damn well bet I want you to explain,' screamed Binz.

'Well, you see, we know that you only want to kill us, and we are not afraid. Not at all afraid. But before we die, we wish to ask that the Camp Commandant (Schwatz) and you read out our individual death sentences to us.'

There was a brief silence that, to the motley group of shabby prisoners seemed endless. Fräulein Binz was speechless. She had not bargained for any form of resistance. She had imagined that these women would go to their deaths as quietly, as happily even, as the last bunch. She had certainly not reckoned with so brief so logical, so fearless an argument coming from a snip of a girl. And Fräulein Binz laughed. She laughed with a mixture of anger and embarrassment. Then she said: 'What the hell are you talking about? Nobody is going to kill you. Who put that stupid idea into your hollow heads? You are simply going to be transported to Gross Rosen, that's all.' (Gross Rosen was a small town not far from Berlin.)

'But,' retorted the nineteen-year-old girl, 'even we know, Fräulein Binz, that Gross Rosen is at this very moment occupied by the Russians.'

'If the Russians are at Gross Rosen, then the Russians are here,' screeched Binz, now furious. But a glint of fear in her eye betrayed her. Instead of flogging Jadzia and any other woman in her path, Binz ordered the whole group back to the block to wait for further orders. It seemed as though the women of Ravensbrück had won their first victory.

No further orders came. The Camp Commandant was now too busy killing off Jews to bother about his 'rabbits'. For Schwatz this was a busy period. Berlin had commanded him to take in train load upon train load of Jews from Auschwitz and to exterminate them as quickly as possible. Auschwitz could not cope with them all. It looked as though time was running out and that the one thousand-year plan would have to be hurried along. If Germany was losing the war — and Schwatz would not allow himself to believe it yet — all traces of torture would have to be eradicated. The dead could tell no tales and the living would have to join the land of the dumb.

On April 23, 1945, Binz called Lydia to her office. She was all smiles. The whip she had always carried about with her as part of her uniform was nowhere to be seen. 'Well, Lipski,' she said and to Lydia, who had only been a number, her name sounded strange to her, 'you are to join some others and leave the camp.'

Lydia braced herself. 'I can only repeat what has already once been said to you, Fräulein Binz and that is that I should like to have my death sentence read out to me officially before going to your ovens.'

Binz blushed. There was no longer any immediate fit of anger in her voice or in her manner. Lydia's words had acted like a slap in the face and Binz let her eyes drop guiltily. 'No,' she said, 'there will be no need for that. It is quite true. You and quite a number of others are to leave here. Please... please (a please from Binz!) do not think too badly of us and what we did to you here in this camp. We were, you understand, only acting on orders, obeying commands.'

Binz held out her hand — her gesture of final defeat. Lydia looked down on the hand stretched out in friendship towards her. Her heart told her to spit at this creature, kick her, kill her just as she had done with defenceless prisoners. But a strange compassion filled her, seeing how quite suddenly the once mighty, once strong Fräulein Binz had changed into a cringing, frightened little animal. Her judgment will come, thought Lydia and, without another word, ignored the outstretched hand, turned on her heel and walked out.

Binz stood alone in her office. She, too, knew her sins would be accounted for. Now she felt very tired, very weak. Her hand fell limply to her hip and she looked with distaste round her office. There stood the desk and the chair from which she had ruled over her prisoners. She would rule no longer.

Above the desk hung the picture of the Fuehrer. His face looked strong, powerful. She had never met him and now her ambition to do so faded. She felt that she had been betrayed. How she had slaved for him and his great Reich — and for what? To what end? To this defeat, this dishonour. Fräulein Binz picked up the heavy ashtray on her desk and flung it with all her remaining might at the picture. Hitler's face, torn and now expressionless lay at her feet. She stamped on the face hysterically, tears streaming down her cheeks.

'*Du Schwein, du altes, dreckiges Schwein! Es ist alles deine Schuld, deine Schuld!*' The words melted with the stamping of her feet and the sobs. The Beast of Ravensbrück had turned into a mouse.*

Lydia was the only 'rabbit' to join a group of 1,200 French, Belgian and Dutch women to leave the camp. Still weak, weighing only sixty-five pounds, she limped her way to the train that waited to take the small, dishevelled army of women away. There were no songs, no cheers. In silence they marched through the gate; in silence they turned to look for the last time towards the chimney of hell, now extinct like some tired volcano. Beneath that chimney, they knew, were the ashes of those they had loved, those they had known for perhaps only a few hours but hours that were as valuable as a whole lifetime.

Lydia looked back towards the rabbit huts that represented the homes for thousands and smelled for the last time the acrid stench of disease and of decaying bodies.

The Swedish Red Cross had taken over the camp. Well-fed, tear-stained men and women helped Lydia and the others board a clean, comfortable train that was to take them across a bleeding, smouldering Germany to Denmark. The world had yet to find out that war did not mean only bombs and killing in the field of battle, but that it also included taking human beings and stripping them of every vestige of self-respect and respect for others, slaughtering them like so many cattle, gassing them, burning them, piling up mountains of flesh and bones into pyramids of horror.

The train moved slowly away from Ravensbrück. Sven Jansen, engine-driver, pulled the cord that let out a whistle of steam. The whistle was a salute to the dead, a sound of hope to the dying, a cry of victory to those still able to walk, talk and think.

The war, the tortures, the murder was over.

Lydia was free. And she joined in with the weeping of joy. She was a child grown into an old woman. She would have to learn how to become a child again, how to find her youth out of the rubble of the past, how to forget her tortures and rebuild her life — the life she had not yet learned to live.

---

* And the mouse was hanged after being found guilty of mass murder at the Nuremberg War Crimes trials.

Somewhere, someone began singing the Marseillaise. Soon the whole train was singing. Outside, the sun broke through grey clouds and shone down on the destruction of a would-be empire. Villages lay burned to the ground; towns were unrecognizable as towns. Only bricks and stones piled high where houses had once stood. Germany was a sorry sight.

In Denmark the train was besieged by the people. They threw their own meagre rations to the 1,200 women, cheered and wept and waved. The language was different but no one needed a dictionary to understand the meaning.

In Sweden, the prisoners were fed and clothed. And Lydia slept. She slept and slept. For three days and three nights she lay in a deep, refreshing healing sleep. And then she was fed again. Each piece of meat tasted like heaven. Few could stomach the rich food at first, few could recall table manners, some fought for slices of bread for they could only remember having to fight for each crumb. And after the banqueting, the women awoke from their nightmares and sang and danced. Lydia, the colour returning to her pale cheeks, repeated the dances she had performed in the camp, accompanied to handclapping and humming.

Rehabilitation Camp they called it. To the inmates it was finer than any hotel in the world. The beds were soft, the doctors were kind and gentle, people smiled. Smiled. Smiles were something of the past, of another world. But then, this was another world to Lydia and her friends.

After a month or so, Lydia was called to the office of the Red Cross official in charge of the Camp.

'Mademoiselle Lipski, please won't you sit down?' He was smiling and indicated an armchair at the side of his desk. Lydia sat, expectant, tense. 'I have some news for you — and I think it will make you feel a lot better. Your father…'

'Papa!' Lydia cried and jumped up. She had given up all hope of ever seeing her father again.

'…is safe and well.'

Lydia stood, mouth wide open in astonishment. After a long silence during which she could hear her heart beating loud and fast, she summoned up the energy to ask: 'Where — oh, please, where is he?'

The Red Cross officer had played these scenes before. Sometimes they were not as happy. Sometimes his news was hard to break. He had told others that their mother or brother, father or sister or husband had been found alive; he should have been used to these reactions by now, but each time was for him a new experience. To give back the past to those who had no hope for the

14. Dance of joy: Ravensbrück's forgotten. Lydia and her friends dance the jitterbug before other liberated prisoners (most of them in this picture are Jews) in Sweden.

future was like breathing life into the dead. He cleared his contracted throat.

'He is in Paris and has already been informed of your whereabouts. We found him at the camp of Mauthausen. You were the first person for whom he asked, Mademoiselle. I am very proud and happy to be able to give you this news. We know all about your father's good work for the Resistance and we are even prouder to have learned about your own work in the Movement. Such courage as yours is rare among people as young as yourself, Mademoiselle. May I be permitted to congratulate you? We shall, of course, do everything in our power to see to it that you are returned to France quickly.'

He went on talking, but Lydia could not hear, could not distinguish his words. Her father was alive. That was all that mattered to her now. Her mind's eye picked up the image of him as she had last seen him. It was not the image of the small man waving to her at the prison of Romainville, but of the kind, happy father, holding her hand as they skipped through woods and fields in the country around La Celle St. Cloud. The official's voice droned

15. Lydia after her liberation from Ravensbrück—sick and weak, but still beautiful.

on in the background, his face distorted and blurred through Lydia's tears. In her mind she repeated the poem she had received from her father when she was at the Santé.

Do not cry, my child, should you see all hopes of happiness
Disappear so suddenly from all your dreams,
For one day soon God Himself will dispel your distress
And give your heart once more the means
To laugh
If love has wounded you and you suffer, alas —
Do not cry.

But if one winter's eve when all is sad
And your soul has suffered and your heart feels low,
Come then, o come to the refuge of my arms.
With love they will be open.
And pressed against me, as of days gone by,
You may cry. Yes, then you may cry.

'Oh, bless you, Monsieur, God bless you,' Lydia cried as the Red Cross officer held out his hand to her.

CHAPTER SIXTEEN:

TO LYDIA, A SON

L ydia was twenty when she arrived at the Swiss convalescent home. In normal circumstances such places are filled with the elderly and the middle aged, resting after a long illness or spending one's riches in retirement in the midst of sunny alpine snows and fresh air. But during the years immediately after the cruel Second World War, such homes were filled to overflowing with young and old alike. The young filled their lungs with the crisp, healing air that made their brittle bones strong again. The old took pleasure in making their last days more enjoyable and rested in the peace of the high mountains and lakes. Lydia was able to eat and sleep and think again. Her lungs, choked with the fumes and the filth of Ravensbrück and spotted with the gnawing germs of tuberculosis, received their much longed-for overhaul as she took her first step along the great journey back to health.

Her reunion with her father had been the most joyful experience in her life. He had looked so thin, so aged and his own story was stamped with so much horror but all the terror of the past was forgotten with their meeting.

He had been saved from the jaws of death at the last moment. Because of his part in the Resistance, he was made to carry out only the most menial tasks at Mauthausen and had been among a group of Poles and Jews that were to be gassed and burned on the day the camp was liberated. During the last year at Mauthausen, the camp's crematorium had turned to ashes 180,000 human beings.

But not all reunions are completely happy. Lydia's mother, Irenka, had died at the hands of the Germans in Poland. Her brother was missing and it was not until two years after the war that the young handsome boy she had only known as a baby returned to France and the family circle.

It was at the convalescent home that Lydia met her first man. With the exception of the boy she had grown to love from a distance at Romainville, she had never been in close contact with any man, let alone fallen in love. At the age of twenty-one, a heroine in the eyes of the French people, a girl who had suffered more than many a man could himself bear, Lydia was still a virgin. Now, in the heavenly peace of Switzerland, she was at last able to think of other things than where the next crust of bread might be coming from or whether she could hold onto life for yet another desperate day. Her passions, having lain dormant for so long, were able at last to awake and become real. The man with whom she fell in love had also floated upon the flotsam of humanity, had also been saved from the gaping jaws of death.

He was tall, gangling, dark and of noble birth. His name: Ludovic de la Chapelle Rozat de Mandres, a Viscount and twenty-three years old. The Germans had arrested him at his home at Grenoble. They had placed him in a forced-workers' group but he had refused to work for the Nazis. His aristocratic French blood had revolted against the invaders. And so he was transported to Belsen. Now they were together, Lydia and Ludovic. It was he who taught her to ski on the slopes of the Swiss Alps. Together they bathed in the warm lakes. Together they strolled through the fields and talked and talked, opening bare their hearts to one another. Their laughter cheered the other patients into the happy will to live. Together they grew handsome and beautiful.

'I love you, Lydia,' Ludovic had told her when they were ready for release as 'fit for duty.'

'No one has ever said that to me before,' Lydia answered. She felt shy and happy. Now that someone held her in his arms, close and tight, she did not know what to do. But she was happy. Ludovic taught her happiness. He taught her love, taught her how to kiss and how to caress. And she gave herself to him willingly that day on the slopes overlooking Chamonix. Now she knew that all her life she had waited for this moment without realizing how beautiful it could be. They made love again and again, catching up on the years they had lost with kisses that were meant to last forever.

Back in Paris they still clung together. They took a small flat high up above the Seine and lived there as man and wife. There had been no marriage ceremony, no church service. But there was nothing sinful in their life. Marriage, man-made marriage, with certificates and signatures, was not for them — not yet. First they wanted to taste the pleasures of love completely as lover and mistress.

One day Vic (Lydia no longer called him Ludovic) ran up the stairs of their house in a state of great excitement. He burst into the room.

'Sweetheart, oh, sweetheart, wonderful news. I've been offered a great job, a fabulous job with an engineering firm....'

'Vic, how wonderful ! Where? With whom?'

'Well, it means leaving France. It's in the Ivory Coast.'

'The Ivory Coast? You mean, we'll have to go to West Africa? Oh, Vic, when do we go?'

Ludovic was silent for a while. The excitement with which he had announced his great news left him and his face became grave.

'Well, darling, you see. I explained about you of course, but... well...'

Lydia tried to make her voice sound natural. 'You mean, I can't come with you, is that what you're trying to tell me? Well, that's all right Vic, darling. I suppose I'd only be in the way....'

'Don't be so silly, Lydia. You know you'd never be in my way. But it's just that I'll have to go out there first. Naturally, I'll send for you as soon as I've settled there. It won't be long, you'll see.'

The last days before Vic's sailing were painful for both of them. And as the eve of his departure drew near, Lydia sunk into long periods of depression. She wept for hours on end. There was something she had to tell him, but how? For a whole week she had kept the news of her pregnancy to herself. At last she summoned up the energy and courage to share the news with the man who was the child's father.

'Vic — I didn't want to tell you this just before you go away, but I think I must ... I went to the doctor the other day and — and....'

Vic ran to her side. 'Darling, you're... we're... oh God, how wonderful! Why didn't you tell me this at once? This is great news, great news!'

Vic was convinced the child would be a boy. It just had to be a boy. He even thought out the names with which the child should be christened and went to the authorities to register the unborn son as his.

And so, while Vic was in Africa, Lydia became bigger and basked in the loneliness of her pregnancy. At 11.30 p.m. on February 7, 1947, Patrick Wladimir Napoléon Marie de la Chapelle Rozat de Mandres came into the world. Patrick, because for some reason Vic had always been fond of the Irish patron saint and Wladimir after Lydia's father.

The reason for Napoléon went with the traditions of the de la Chapelle family whose ancestors were at the court of Napoléon III. But Lydia's happiness in her son was dampened by the unhappiness in her heart. Vic returned from Africa two years later, both his lungs severely hit by

16. The post-war Lydia and her son Patrick aged two. It was the first time his father, Vic, had seen him, having just returned from Africa.

tuberculosis. Lydia wanted to marry him at once, care for him, love him. But Vic refused. He would not, he said, want to be a burden to her and their child. When he was recovered, he said, he would then marry her gladly. So Lydia had to work for all three of them, and when her grandmother, old and gentle joined the household, there were four mouths to feed.

Lydia's return to Paris did not go unnoticed. Her tremendous work as a child in the Resistance alongside her father had never been forgotten and she was immediately awarded a Croix de Guerre first class by General de Gaulle himself. Her bravery, both during the German occupation of France and throughout her nightmare life in prison as well as Ravensbrück, was recounted in the French Press. Medals of one kind and another were heaped upon her by various organizations that had been involved in the fight against the Nazi occupation. The climax came in 1960 when the Maréchal Juin made her a Chevalier of the Légion d'Honneur – just about the most high-ranking medal that could be awarded in France. Lydia is still ranked as the most decorated woman in the country.

But honour-filled medals do not produce food for empty stomachs. In order to make some little money, Lydia took part in galas to aid deported ex-prisoners. These galas were held regularly and the artists taking part were all concentration camp graduates themselves. It was at one of these galas, after Lydia had danced to her own choreography, that she was approached by Madame Zoula de Bonza of the *Opéra Comique*, Paris.

'*Mon enfant*, you have great talent,' said Madame de Bonza. 'Of course, you have inherited it from your dear departed mother. Oh, yes, I knew her very well. Irenka, may the good Lord preserve her soul, and I used to dance together. Ah, you should have heard the applause then. It was like a thunder-claps. And the cheering. Ah, the audiences of old were wonderful. Not like these stiff, mamby-pamby people of today. No appreciation of art, that's what it is.'

Madame de Bonza taught ballet and offered to teach Lydia all the finer points of the dance. For several months Lydia slaved under the watchful and experienced eye of this fine old woman. And then, one day, she introduced Lydia to a Monsieur Golding, late director of the A.B.C., one of the leading Paris music halls. Golding looked Lydia up and down.

'Zoula, you're a miracle!' he exclaimed after a short scrutiny of a very embarrassed, very nervous Lydia. 'Where on earth did you find her? And why did you not show her to me before? Such lovely legs and such a beautiful body should not be kept hidden, Zoula.'

'Oh, for goodness' sake stop talking about the girl as though she is some pedigree dog or race horse,' shouted Madame de Bonza good naturedly. 'She is a girl of great talent and she can dance, really dance — not like many of those elephants you've got at that theatre of yours you old rascal. I've taught her — though I must admit, I didn't need to teach her much. It's in her blood. Her mother was a great dancer, you know. Well, what d'you say? Will you give my little Lydia a chance?'

Golding engaged Lydia on the spot. She was to take part in the show that brought back one of the greatest old-timers of the Paris music-hall — Mistinguette. On the opening night, everyone that was anyone was in the audience. *Le Tout Paris* was there. Maurice Chevalier sat out front together with Paul Derval, director of the Folies-Bergère, and the fourth 'name' in French showbusiness — Josephine Baker.

17. General Masson presents Lydia with the Légion d'Honneur.

18. The day Lydia received her Croix de Guerre (January 22, 1946) presented to her by General Larminat.

19. *Extract from the Decree of Lydia's Légion d'Honneur dated November 13, 1959, a knighthood rank signed by Charlet de Gaulle, President of the French Republic and by Prime Minister Michel Debre.*

20. *Extract from the document of Lydia's Croix de Guerre dated November 10, 1945, and signed by General de Gaulle, and by General Juin.*

21. At her father's Paris home

22. The day Lydia received her Légion d'Honneur (March 12,1960)—and a kiss from her son Patrick.

The show was a success. Mistinguette sang all her old songs and some new ones and showed those fabulous legs of hers. The French loved her — but the flame had gone dim in the old woman. In the background, new talent was easily discernible. And Lydia de Lipski was noticed.

Paul Derval turned to his right-hand man Michel Gyarmathy, artistic director of the Folies and said: 'Do you see what I see?' Gyarmathy had already taken note of the young girl who was dancing so beautifully and looked at his programme. Lydia Lipski? Was this not the girl who had been decorated by Général de Gaulle and the Maréchal Juin? Was this the same girl as the one who held the rank of Lieutenant of the Resistance? Gyarmathy was determined to find out.

Gyarmathy, himself a Hungarian Jew, was born on January 23, 1908 as Miklos Ehrenfeld. He decided to go to France when he was about 22 and settled in Paris in 1933. He was a talented artist and writer and joined the Folies-Bergère shortly after his arrival in the French capital. He was probably the best thing to have happened to that theatre in its entire history. Thanks to him, the Folies became the legend with which it is associated throughout the world. He designed the sets, wrote the scenarios, produced the shows, composed the music, and selected the best looking young women in the business.

Gyarmathy engaged Lydia for the Folies as soon as the Mistinguette show came off. Lydia became a part of the great Folies on April 1, 1950 and was an instant success.

And yet with the Folies also came despair and anguish. At home, Lydia's horrors started anew. On joining the Folies, her name had been changed to Lova. Lydia Lova was felt to be a good stage name. The Folies did not go in for 'gimmicks'. They did not want to use Lydia's past and present fame for publicity purposes. So she became Lydia Lova, dancer. And nude dancer at that.

'I see nothing wrong in showing off one's body if it is worth showing,' she said at the time. 'And at the Folies-Bergère, the body is used to artistic ends. There is nothing ugly or dirty about it. The girls at the theatre take their job seriously and if men like to look at them, well, so much the better.'

But Ludovic, who was still unable to work, grew bored with sitting at home, living off Lydia and waiting for her return every night. He grew angry and jealous. Until now he had done nothing to help support the 'family'. He had made no attempt to marry Lydia. He was forced to accept the money she earned but jealous of the way in which she earned it.

'What sort of a life do you think this is you're leading?' he would storm at her. 'Taking off your clothes in front of a lot of greasy old men? Why in hell should they have the right to see your body?'

There were brawls; angry arguments; fights. Lydia was used to beatings but when they came from the man she loved, they hurt more than any of the kicks she had received from her Nazi tormentors.

And the greatest horror of all was that Lydia had no legal right to her son. This was and continued to be the strange injustice of French law. Without going through a lengthy and expensive legal battle, Pat could never be completely hers. She had given birth to him, yet his father had registered his rights as father. It is the father who remained responsible for his upbringing and pay for his schooling. And Pat bore his father's name – and his mother's love.

The fights and the brawls became more and more frequent. Till, in the early 'fifties, Ludovic disappeared. He left the flat without a farewell, without a note, without a word of love.

Although Pat rarely saw his father, it was Ludovic who paid his schooling at the exclusive boarding school near Rambouillet, where French presidents have their traditional presidential country residence. Pat saw his mother only once a fortnight. He never really understood the complicated intricacies in which he was entangled. He only came to realize them later, much later, only then was he able to join his mother and grandfather on their holidays. He became the apple of Wladimir de Korczac Lipski's eye and took after granddad as a poet.*

His talents as an artist became remarkable and he painted some very fine canvases. He, at least, appreciated what his mother was doing and even went to shows at the Folies-Bergère to see and applaud her.

And what shows they were! Lydia was always the first artist to replace anyone who was off sick — including the stars of the show. She understudied such stars as Veronica Bell, Colette Floriot and Yvonne Menard; she took part in sketches with the great, late comedian, Dandy, and she sang with Randall — even in English, a language with which she was only very barely acquainted. But above all, she danced her way to the top.

Yet each night, when she returned wearily to her flat high up in the rue Hegesippe-Moreau in Pigalle, the nightmares of her past returned to her and she would often wake up in a cold sweat.

One thought continued to haunt her – that injection she was given at Ravensbrück along with the prediction that its effects would not be noticed for some 25 years. Lydia used to get the odd shiver down her spine but if

---

* Two of Patrick's poems appear in Appendix One.

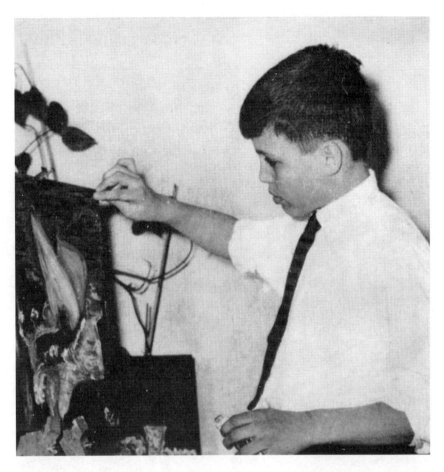

23. Patrick the Painter: he inherits the talent from his mother.

the injection was having any effect, it was not noticed by her. She visited a number of eminent doctors who took numerous blood tests to analyse her, but nothing of any significance showed up. As far as the medical profession was concerned, Lydia Lova was perfectly clear.

No one had bothered to look at some old records of similar time lags. There was the example of a British soldier who was stationed in Egypt during the First World War and who accidentally fell into the Sweetwater Canal, which now runs alongside the Suez Canal and is probably the most misnamed stretch of water in the Middle East. Animals die in it; local humans use it as a lavatory; it looks beautiful but is filled with deadly dangers. While the British

23, 24, 25, 26 At home and at the Folies

27 Place Blanche—the nearest Metro

still occupied the Canal Zone, soldiers who fell into the Sweetwater Canal had to be injected with many different types of antibiotic or face very serious consequences. The First World War soldier received no such injections and felt perfectly all right until a strange illness brought him down – just before the Second World War. Doctors took many blood tests but found nothing of consequence. At last he was sent into the Hospital for Tropical Diseases where doctors questioned him very closely. He told them of his Egyptian experience – and his swim in the Sweetwater Canal. He was cured – nearly thirty years after the event.

Lydia Lova continued to dance at the Folies and even came to London for a three-week contract with the Casino de Paris strip club, where she was a resounding success. But fate caught up with her one weekend in 1966, shortly after her forty-first birthday. She had ended her 'dance with the devil' at the Folies-Bergère to rapturous applause and a standing ovation of cheers and had made her way home. In her apartment, she suddenly found it hard to breathe and opened the window. But the breathing became so bad that she began to choke. She managed to get to the phone and call an ambulance. She was rushed to hospital. By the Monday morning, Lydia was dead. Doctors could do nothing to save her. They diagnosed cancer but no one was completely sure.

Death had come twenty-three years after that concentration camp injection. The Devil had taken this beautiful heroine at the age of forty-one. It was a hollow victory.

APPENDIX ONE

The following is a selection of poems written by Wladimir de Korczac Lipski, Lydia Lova's father, at the prisons of Fresnes and Romainville and the concentration camp Mauthausen. The first, dedicated to Lydia, was written in the darkness of October 1942 at Fresnes, where Lipski occupied the cell reserved for those condemned to death.

Danse pour moi!

Quand dans le mois de Mai s'eveille la nature,
Que dans les champs tout pousse et s'anime et tout croit,
Danse parmi les fleurs et parmi la verdure,
Du beau Printemps de Grieg, tout l'amour et la joie,
Quand par un soir d'été, aux fleuves troublantes,
Je rêve au fond du parc, tout rempli de senteurs,
Danse, au clair de lune, une valse très lente,
Qui alanguit les sens et rapproche les coeurs.
Et quand l'automne est là, sur le pas de nos portes,
Que le soleil, le moms chaud, a des reflects de sang,
Sur les bords du grand lac, parmi les feuilles mortes,
Danse pour moi, veux tu, le 'Cygne' de Saint Saens.
Quand dans les nuits d'hiver, le vent souffle en rafale,
Que des flocons tout blancs, ont couvert les grand pins;
Devant l'âtre embrasé, sous sa clarté d'or pale,
Danse avec ferveur, sur des airs de Chopin.
Quand au printemps, je sens que mon coeur bat plus vite,
Que j'ai dans les poumons tout l'air pur des grands bois,
Danse, sans hèsiter pour moi, chère petite,
La 'Czardas' de Monti, ou bien sa Mazurka.
Et quand, dans mon studio je rime et je compose,
Cherchant la vèrité, la grâce et la beauté,
L'harmonie d'une ligne, un geste ou une pose,
Danse 'Maestro Please' afin de m'inspirer.
Et quand le soir descend sous un ciel de tropiques
Et qu'une brise vient calmer la terre en feu,
Parmi les orangers et les fleurs exotiques.
Danse avec ardeur un tango voluptueux.
Et au temps des moissons quand l'amour se promène,

[182]

Que partout les sentiers sont tout pleins d'amoureux;
Au rythme langoureux d'une valse de Vienne,
Danse pour me charmer ton beau Danube Bleu.
Lorsque le laboureur a jeté sa semence,
Que les jours sont moms longs et que tombe la pluie,
Dans ta robe de cour avec majesté danse
Sur l'air du Menuet que fit Borricelli.
Et puis quand les grands froids ont engourdi la terre,
Que je me sens tout triste et que mon coeur est las;
Avec des gestes lents, incarnant la Prière,
Danse de Gounod, pour moi, l'Ave Maria.
Et quand enfin mes yeux s'empliront de ténèbres,
Que je m'endormirai d'un sommeil éternel,
Danse sur l'air sacré de la Marche Funèbre,
Pour mieux guider mes pas sur la route de ciel.

This next poem has been set to music and performed for the first time by
Lyne de Souza of the Folies-Bergère. The simplicity of the repetition and the
balance make this little masterpiece lend itself easily to the *Lieder* school. It
was written at the fortress prison of Romainville in January, 1943.

Les Saisons

Quand au printemps Phoebus vient réchauffer la terre,
Eveiller doucement la nature endormie,
Et qu'Eros soulevant le voile du mystère,
Vient féconder le monde et lui donner la vie
Pour mieux fèter l'amour et les joies qu'll enfante —
       Je chante.
Quand par on soir d'été la vague enfin clémente
Sur la plage ensablée vient mollement mourir,
Je poursuis sur les flots une chimère ardente
Que laissa dans mon coeur un lointain souvenir
Pour prolonger encore cette impression trop brève —
       Je rêve.

Quand de son voile triste et lugubre d'automne
Couvre les bois de brume et les chemins de bone,
Que la pluie stir les toits tombe et bruit monotone,
J'erre dans le grand parc sur le sol froid et mou,

Et quand je rentre enfin, très las, dans ma demeure —
        Je pleure.
Lorsque l'hiver, glacial, le vent souffle en tempête,
Que le sol est couvert d'un grand linceul tout blanc,
Que dans l'ombre tapie, la mort sournoise guette
Et ouvre tout à coup les portes du Néant,
Quand en hurlant le vent sous ma porte s'engouffre —
        Je souffre.
Mais quand parfois je vois dans la nuit froide et sombre,
Le ciel bleu constelle de male astres brillants,
Et que je sens ta main serrant ma main dans l'ombre
Et combien le Bon Dieu protège les amants,
Sondant de l'infini le passionant mystere —
        J'espère

To be able to see so many horrors and still keep one's wit — even one's true sense of humour — must indeed be difficult. Wladimir de Korczac Lipski wrote many poems during his time at Mauthausen. Most of them were filled with sadness, even if they did call for hope for the future and encouraged other prisoners to resist death and the Germans. However, the following little gem was written at the concentration camp one evening in March, 1945. The war was almost at an end, admittedly, and it is perhaps because de Lipski sensed the closeness of the liberation that he managed to inject so much joy, so much humour into this poem which, like the last, has been set to music and was performed first by Fanny Marette of the Amabassadeurs, Paris.

La Femme

Quand Dieu cut façonné de sa main géniale
La femme, modèle d'art et de perfection,
Il contempla longtemps son oeuvre idéale
Et c'est là que naquit la première émotion.
Puis ayant animé cette forme immobile
Il la dota alors des plus pures vertues
Il lui donna un coeur délicat et fragile
Une âme dont l'éclat lui parut absolu.
Et tout semblait parfait dans l'oeuvre ravissante!…
Mais le front du Seigneur soudain devint soucieux…
Quelque chose manquait à l'idole charmante…
Une lente harmonie entre l'âme et les yeux
Et c'est alors que Dieu en sa bonté immense

Pour rendre immortelle la déesse achevée,
A la femme donna sa sublime puissance:
Il lui confia l'amour et lui permit d'aimer.

Lydia's son, Patrick, who had already written some highly advanced, mature and sensitive poetry while he was still a mere teenager, has his moments of humour as well. Here is a little ditty he penned in Paris in 1961 when he was fourteen. It concerns two cats called:

Minet et Minette

Minet aimait Minette — mais Minette portait des lunettes
Et Minet de s'affoler, et joie à Minette pour miauler,
Minet ne mangeait guère de rats — Minet, chat de goutière,
Logeait en un creux de cuisinière.
Le beau jour vint que Minet s'en alla faire cour après
    Minette .
Depuis ce jour, Minette
Mit au monde des goutières angorats.

This humour is however only found in Patrick's poems (he signs himself 'Patt') when he was in Paris together with his mother. When he was further afield, holidaying with his school or with his father, he sent Lydia poems that cry out with longing. The following is such a sample. It was written at Montfort l'Amaury in 1961.

Les Regrets....

Je suis triste, hélàs!
Loin de vous je me lasse,
Perdu dans la brume en fuyant,
Je pense à ce passé charmant
Quand tous les quatre pres de l'âtre
Où vassillait la flamme folâtre
Nous la regardions longuement.
Elle chantait, gémissait en brûlant.
Voilà, ami, où j'en suis,
Comme la colombe loin de son nid,
Rêve perdu, lueure étouffée,
Cela n'est qu'un passé.

APPENDIX TWO

Lydia Lova, nude dancer of the Folies-Bergère, did not jump into the spotlight immediately. True, Michel Gyarmathy had recognized her talents — as did Paul Derval — the moment he saw her dancing in the Mistinguette revue at the A.B.C. They both realized that here they had found a girl who had the talent required at the Folies — good looks, a perfect figure, the will to work hard and a personality that shone through every step of her dancing, every gesture of her hands and arms.

But it is not all that easy at the Folies. Some of the 'girls' had been on that vast stage for fifteen years — yet have still not found their way to the neon-lit credits above the front door. Yet each girl was chosen carefully by Gyarmathy. Each girl was put through her paces. So were the stars of the show. Whether the name was Josephine Baker or Maurice Chevalier — or Lydia Lova: each was made to work. If they did not put their heart and soul into a routine that had to be repeated three hundred and sixty-five times a year for three, maybe four years, they were given their cards without much ceremony. Gyarmathy did not stand for any nonsense, any shirking.

Lydia Lova had her big chance through another's misfortunes, as is so often the case nowadays. The year was 1958 and the star of the Folies was the beautiful Yvonne Menard. Yvonne had everything. Audiences cheered her until they were hoarse. Men fought amongst themselves to book the best seats in the house.

The theatre was packed to capacity every night. Everyone who was anyone had come to see 'Folies Légères'. Yvonne Menard was known as the Empress of Undress. Shortly before she had opened at the Folies, she had made a triumphant tour of the United States. Americans invaded the Paris theatre as though Yvonne was a local girl from back home. They knew her, loved her. The French threw her carpets of roses at the end of each night's performance. Here was a star indeed!

Paul Derval told Jean Marais, the French film actor, after the latter had burst into Mademoiselle Menard's dressing-room one night to throw his arms around her and congratulate her: 'I can well realize why all these people have taken her to their hearts. She is so complete (un tout). She is like Mistinguette. She is like Josephine Baker (whom she had succeeded). She can dance. She can sing. When necessary, she can even act the fool in some of our sketches.'

She was, indeed, hard to replace. And the day Yvonne Menard attempted suicide, both Paul Derval and Michel Gyarmathy had a gigantic problem to solve.

*28 The day
Lydia had her
big chance:
replacing
Folies star
Yvonne Menard.*

*29. The Proud
Heroine.*

30. At the Folies.

Yvonne Menard was everything. And perhaps because of this, she was too much, did too many things. She had lost weight, found it more and more difficult to sleep at night after even so tiring a performance as hers and suffered headache upon headache. Each night she was besieged by autograph hunters. Once, three English tourists in high spirits had tried to kidnap her. It all became too much. The girl who had reached the summit of her career one night decided to end it. After the show, she climbed into her sleek sports car and drove off at ninety miles an hour to her exotic studio in the rue Pierre Grenier.

She had read in some book or other that the Romans used to lie in their baths and cut their arteries when committing suicide. Apparently, lying in the water brought death more swiftly and more comfortably.

Yvonne was discovered, however, before it was too late. The concierge had come up with some telegrams — they arrived at all hours of the day and night — received no reply to her knocks and calls and could hear Yvonne's alsatian whining pitifully inside the apartment.

Gyarmathy and Derval spent all night and the rest of the next day choosing a girl to replace her. Lydia was awakened in the early hours of the morning and ordered to come to the theatre at once.

'We want to try you out in some of Yvonne's numbers,' she was told by Gyarmathy abruptly, impatiently. Somewhere a piano played a familiar melody and Lydia, without knowing the facts behind this extraordinary decision, danced.

Gyarmathy was not disappointed. Lydia replaced Yvonne.

'But it was not quite as simple as that,' said Paul Duval. 'Yvonne Menard also had a voice, and, alas, Lydia — well, she could sing, sure, but she was no operatic sensation. We had to choose two girls to replace the one. We picked one out from thirty likely ones in the show — a little blonde called Micheline Roine. It was no great surprise to either Michel or myself that when the hospital (the Boucicaut Hospital) called for blood donors to save Yvonne's life, Lydia and Micheline were first in the queue.'

APPENDIX THREE

Mathilde alias Micheline Carré alias La Chatte – The Cat – was without doubt one of the most interesting, if not *the* most interesting double agent of the Second World War. She possessed other names as well. After her birth at midnight on June 29, 1908 at Le Creusot, a pretty little town that nestled close to the Saône-et-Loire, she was christened Mathilde-Lucie Bélard. Some friends called her Lily; others, Micheline. Her family, the Bélards, had come to France from Spain in 1765.

One thing became rapidly clear: Mathilde was a highly intelligent child and soared to the top of every class she entered throughout her school years. She passed her Baccalauréat with honours and was admitted to the Sorbonne, the University of Paris, where she studied modern languages in order to become a teacher. It was the profession she had yearned for ever since she was a pupil at her first primary school in the Jura mountains.

In 1932, Mademoiselle Mathilde Bélard was appointed assistant teacher at a small primary school in Paris, where her first day, like the first day of virtually any new teacher, was hectic. She had been put in charge of a class of fifty rowdy youngsters, most of them back-street urchins. The noise in that classroom grew louder and louder so that it finally attracted the teacher from next door, who turned out to be an exceptionally attractive young man named Maurice Carré. The two immediately struck up a close relationship and a year later, on May 18, 1933, they were secretly married.

After a short honeymoon in Italy, they moved to Algeria, where they found teaching jobs at the Ain-Sefra School near Oran. Mathilde taught Muslim children aged six to eight to read and write French. Both she and Maurice were deliriously happy – but this was not to last for very long. War had been declared and threw everything into turmoil. The couple packed their bags and returned to Paris but were soon separated by the sudden rush of refugees from the French capital.

Maurice returned to Ain-Sefra but could not find his wife. He wrote letter after letter to every member of the Bélard family without success. He even wrote an urgent personal letter to Maréchal Petain in his attempt to trace Mathilde, but there was still nothing. In desperation, he joined the Army, was rapidly commissioned to the rank of Lieutenant and became one of the first fatalities of the war.

By the time Maurice fought the invading Germans, Mathilde-Lucie Lily Micheline (Micheline was to become her *nom de guerre*) was already well into her training towards becoming La Chatte. She had witnessed the fall of France to Germany in 1940 and had immediately joined the French Resistance. She also chose to embrace her second favourite profession – nursing.

And she also fell deeply in love for the second time – with a Pole called Roman Czerniewski who in the Resistance movement went by the name of Armand. They made an excellent team. Nurse Carré had managed to make close contacts with members of the Vichy Second Bureau and, thanks to Armand, was also able to join the Franco-Polish espionage network, which was conveniently based in Paris.

The new partnership proved to be excellent in that it managed to organise a brilliant network of agents stationed in towns and villages throughout France. The agents passed messages pinpointing the whereabouts of German military strengths to the London-based Polish Government in exile. The movements of German troops and tanks, the growth of German munitions factories as well as the development of enemy airfields within Normandy, proved most helpful to the Polish network and the War Office in London.

All Resistance workers were provided with pseudonyms but none of them was as appropriate as that of the stealthy, feline Mathilde. Without even realising what was happening, she and Armand had managed to throw open the doors to espionage.

But the network was not only highly useful to the Polish London-based branch, but also to the wider French Resistance Movement. Vital messages and plans were regularly exchanged between Mathilde or her agents and the Korczak Lipskis -- Wladimir and Lydia.

La Chatte proved to be an excellent resistance worker who earned the respect of both French and British political leaders. She had formed a special group in Paris, known as the *Interallié*. She regularly radioed messages to Britain giving details of enemy installations, names and whereabouts of important Nazi officers and so on. London thought highly of her.

When towards the end of 1941, she reached the age of 32, she was suddenly arrested. How this happened is worth retelling. A newly recruited agent to the Franco-Polish network named 'Emile' casually met a German soldier in a small bar in Cherbourg. The German turned out to be nicer than most and a number of drinks were poured and happily consumed. It was possible that 'Emile' had imbibed more than he should have done and he certainly spoke a great deal more than he should have done, including his own part within the Resistance. He casually mentioned the 'boss' who was known as La Chatte. The German naturally passed on the information with more than some glee and it came to the eager ears of Herr Hugo Bleicher who immediately sought the help of the Gestapo and managed to arrest a number of agents within Normandy. One attractive woman who bore the name of 'Violette' (full name: Renée Borni) managed under severe duress to mention someone called Mathilde Carré – also known as La Chatte.

It was the first time that Mathilde had encountered Hugo Bleicher. To her surprise, he did not resort to immediate torture. He recognised in her the potentials of a great agent, possibly the greatest since Mata Hari -- who could be useful to the Third Reich. He also knew that he could persuade her to join his side by threatening to have her shot and to have her parents deported to a concentration camp. She knew that he would carry out his threats and that it was no use trying to wriggle her way out of his trap. So she reluctantly agreed to help him.

Her help proved valuable for Bleicher was able to make 150 arrests – among them the leader of "F1" – Wladimir de Korczac Lipski – and his daughter Lydia. Of the 150, only 30 returned alive to France after the war; the remaining 120 met their deaths in one or other of the many Nazi concentration camps.

It is no secret that she and Bleicher became lovers and that during their lovemaking, she persuaded him to suggest to his superiors that they should send her to London, where she could easily manage to infiltrate the Special Operations Executive (SOE). The Germans did send her to London where she was immediately arrested and closely questioned by the MI5 about the *Abwehr* (German military intelligence – the virtual equivalent of MI5) and its techniques. Fortunately, the British interrogators were more intelligent than their German counterparts, for they had grown suspicious of the attractive Mathilde. They asked her more relevant questions and discovered her little plan to act as a double agent. So she was quietly locked into a cell at Holloway Prison and spent the rest of the war in yet another cell – at Aylesbury Prison. While there, she continued her espionage by acting as a 'snitch' and informing on the activities of other prisoners.

At the end of the war, she was returned to France to face charges of treason. Her trial opened on January 3, 1949 and lasted just four days. During those days, she heard the evidence against her from those few who had managed to evade death. Lydia Lipski and her father were among the chief witnesses for the prosecution. On January 7, 1949, she was sentenced to death.

Fortunately for her, the judge, Maître Albert Naud, believed that there were too many attenuating circumstances to warrant a death sentence and he refused to close the Carré file 'until further notice'. La Chatte continued to sit in her cell, unable to sleep because the guards had refused to turn off her lights. She asked for a Holy Bible to be brought to her. Instead, she was handed an English crime novel. The title: *Condemned to Death*.

Three months later, on April 28, 1949, she was sentenced to death again – but this was almost immediately commuted to a life sentence with hard labour.

Her dreadful tale is brilliantly retold by Gordon Young in his wonderful biography: *The Cat with Two Faces*. 'Those who judged me never knew me,' she said later and added: 'They had never even seen me before I was judged on my manner, my attitude, my smile – a smile of which I was never even conscious.' Yet her counsel continued to fight for her life.

Three years later, when France was beginning to forget its dreadful wounds and was starting to taste prosperity again, her sentence was again changed to twenty years hard labour. That night she wrote in her diary: 'I dreamed that I was in the middle of an ocean. There were battleships all round me. I could see in the distance the sands of the shore. Oh, how I wanted to reach that shore. All of a sudden, I saw a large land that reached out through the mist. It stretched towards me. And I walked on the waters. The water carried me easily and I managed to walk without any difficulty. And I reached the shore'.

Perhaps it was that dream that made the Cat turn to religion. Perhaps it was because mankind had shown her mercy. But on June 27, 1953, the girl who became a double agent for Germany and for England asked to be baptised. The ceremony was held in the greatest secrecy.

On May 18, 1954, her sentence was again reduced – to seven years. That same year, on September 7, Mathilde Carré was freed. The woman they called The Cat tried at first to live in Paris but was unable to keep her presence a secret. The Press and the eyes of neighbours never ceased to invade her privacy. Even Bleicher returned and proposed that they should collaborate on a book of their escapades. Mathilde Carré would have none of it. Instead, she moved as far away as possible from the French capital – 500 miles away – to live like a hermit in the midst of nature, the nature she had never previously tried to understand.

'At last I have found my peace and solitude with God,' she wrote. 'At 54 I have returned to that little child who in her day loved everyone and found beauty in everything.'

Many books have been written around her and about her. Francoise Arnoul played her in the film *La Chatte*.

But Mathilde-Lucie Micheline Lily Carré, née Bélard, turned her back upon books, films and the world, The Cat went home to lick her paws and sleep in the shade of a setting sun. On May 30, 2007, she died quietly in the 6ème Arrondissement of Paris, having reached the ripe old age of 98. Just one more month would have seen her celebrate her 99th birthday on June 30, 2008.